I'M WITH ME

A MEMOIR

MINDY TSAI

I'm with Me: A Memoir

Published by Etcetera Books
Brookline, MA 02445

ISBN: 978-0-578-99601-1 (paperback)
ISBN: 978-0-578-99602-8 (ebook)
LCCN: 2021919320

rev202101

For Robert,
the rock of my life

AUTHOR'S NOTE

I wanted it to work out with every one of the thirty-five men I dated over a period of six years. Starting to date again at the age of forty-one was awkward. Too old to have babies and start a family. Too set in my ways to stop reading *Twilight* and pretend I watch the New England Patriots. Regardless, I was very optimistic, even though I'd never focused my life on dating before and didn't always know what was best to do.

I had two serious relationships in my twenties: Chris and Oliver. Two men who held a special place in my heart, even though I would never name any of my kids after them if I had any. I had high regard for them—both smart, caring, and good-looking. I even thought that since I had them in my life and gave them up, I shouldn't expect to meet anyone else. I had used up all my good karma.

Rachel and Michael, my lifelong friends with happy marriages and children, nudged me toward dating. Having an open mind, I welcomed this challenge and gave it my all, but putting effort into it didn't guarantee me a man. Dating didn't work like a job interview. No job description to read and prepare for. Instead, these thirty-five men held up a mirror in front of my face: "Who are you? Why are you here? What's missing in your life? What are you looking for?"

In this memoir, I chart a different course for single women. Mine is the lesser-told story of a forty-six-year-old woman who does not need marriage or children to be happy. Most of my friends follow more traditional paths. I know many wonderful couples with beautiful children. They have dated, found love, and are nurturing long-term relationships daily. They give their all to raising good kids and to nourishing their marriage. From the outside, their lives look perfect and meaningful, but I have learned that despite all they have, some of them privately envy the life I have. I'm not suggesting my path is better than theirs, but I'm living proof that a woman can lead a fulfilling life not doing what's most accepted and therefore generally thought of as the ideal. There's more than one right way to go through life.

Stories about the actual men I've dated have been altered, combined, or condensed.

CONTENTS

PROLOGUE

I sat at the end of the bed in our quiet, dark room getting ready to go to sleep. As I changed into my pajamas, my arms crossed in front of me when I took off my shirt. My left arm brushed against my left breast, and I felt something as hard as a rock. An electric current went through my body immediately and automatically. *What is that?* I put down both my arms. I touched the spot again and felt the rock. *Do I have cancer? Am I going to die? Should I quit my job tomorrow?* I had to wake my boyfriend, Chris, and turn on the bedside lamp. As I sat there in shock and silence, Chris got help. Within minutes, he dialed a nurse hotline to ask what I should do. Shortly after that discovery, on a workday, Chris drove me to Mt. Auburn Hospital in a blizzard, and I had a biopsy. My heart beating frantically felt like a tiny storm too.

A few days later, I received an inconclusive result from the biopsy. The doctor recommended surgery. Chris took me back to the hospital for the one-day procedure. I was told to change into hospital clothes. I thought the gown's pink color felt cheerful. The clean, spare waiting room had chairs in a circle. I took the only empty seat. A few people talked to each other in soft voices. Someone called my name, and I followed her to a room.

"Just lie down here," she said, pointing to what looked like a bed covered with one of those sterile sheets of paper. A nurse put a needle into my arm. For a few seconds, I felt something cut into my chest even though I didn't feel any pain, just the heaviness of whatever it was on me. The next thing I knew, I woke up in the waiting room. Chris picked me up. The "rock" that had been surgically removed and tested turned out to be a benign cyst about the size of my fist, the doctor told me during the follow-up appointment.

All I had to do after that was take a couple of days off from work and let Chris take care of me while I spent my time mostly on the sofa. Friends sent flowers. At the end of it all, at age twenty-three, the start of my adult life, I was fine. The only thing that remained from this incident was a tiny scar.

Since that experience, and as I've gone through more life changes, I have told myself, "Nobody knows what will happen tomorrow, so live today."

— Part 1 —

RESTART

1

A TASTELESS GARDEN BURGER

On a Wednesday night, I couldn't wait to wrap up work. I worked from home on purpose so I didn't have to spend an hour and a half commuting. I had a first date at six thirty that evening with Adam at a popular restaurant near where I lived. We'd met on an online dating website. We'd texted and exchanged short messages and photos for about three weeks. He said good morning and checked in every day, asking how I was. He'd been kind and sounded friendly when we messaged. I thought he looked cute in his photos: he kept his hair short and clean; his body was fit and tanned.

I got off my laptop and stopped working promptly at five so I could get ready properly. Hoping no one from the office was looking for me, I took a hot shower and then put on my favorite floral dress, pearl earrings, and a matching necklace, which always made me joyous. I'd gotten many compliments wearing this strappy dress that fell just above my knees. The simple, tiny white pearls looked classy and not pretentious.

I didn't wear makeup as I preferred a natural look, but I straightened my long black hair, which I only did when I felt something special might happen. I wanted to look my best.

Adam in a nutshell: fifty years old, eight years older than me. He'd joined the military at nineteen, had been a medic, and was a firefighter when not in service. He'd married in his twenties, had two children, and then divorced and was raising his granddaughter alone. He lived only ten miles from me—a thirty-minute drive, according to Google.

As our online relationship progressed, I learned something quite unexpected: we voted for—take a deep breath—presidential candidates of opposing sides. He told me he would always follow his commander in chief. I tried to be open-minded. I had not noticed any warning signs based on his texts, and I wanted to meet him. I looked forward to intimate conversations about our values, families, America, and the world. I imagined him fighting fires for neighbors and saving lives in wars.

He was reluctant to make plans, which should have set off alarm bells. He always had a full plate taking care of his granddaughter, serving the country, and being stationed at his firehouse—all worthy priorities. I thought at one point we didn't have a chance, but we eventually made plans—at last!

It took less than ten minutes to walk to the restaurant. I arrived at the Publick House in Washington Square fifteen minutes earlier than our agreed time. I stood next to the bar and settled into waiting mode. It was hard to contain my excitement about meeting someone new. Publick House teemed with people, as usual. Men and women packed around tables and lined up tightly along the bar. The whole place echoed different conversations. I felt the energy from the room. Almost everyone had a glass of beer in hand. After all, the place was renowned for its large collection of beers. I'd even been told that only beer snobs came there. I thought Adam might like this place. I figured he might be a beer drinker, which was why I'd suggested we meet there. I stood visibly in front of the entrance next to the host. I looked at the face of every man who walked in, not quite sure I'd recognize Adam easily. Fifteen minutes passed. Then thirty. No one showed up. *Maybe he got caught up with something. I'll give him a bit more time.* An hour later, I decided to grab a corner seat at the end of the bar and ordered a garden burger. I might as well eat. I didn't enjoy the burger but ate it anyway. I no longer felt the energy or heard the sounds in the restaurant. I put away my phone, no longer caring about any incoming text. Two hours after the meeting time, after I finished my food and drink, and after I thought I'd waited long enough, I got up and walked home. Once outside, the air felt especially chilly.

For the first time in my life, at the age of forty-two, someone had stood me up. *What happened to him? He'd better have a really good reason!* When I got home, I did what I always do when I felt emotionally unsteady because of a guy. I emailed Rachel.

"I'm home. Safe. He didn't show," I wrote.

"Unreal. What an ass! Sorry you had to go through the effort, but sounds like another bullet dodged. Seriously, how do people like that even get close to procreation? I was never a fan of this one," Rachel wrote back right away. She was like a sister to me and always more protective of me than I was when it came to my online dating. A successful business-woman running her own company, Rachel had an Ivy League education, a loving husband, and three adorable children, and she volunteered at Rosie's Place, the first women's shelter in the United States. I had seen her through schools, jobs, boyfriends, a wedding, and childbirth. She saw red flags in men so much faster than I was willing or able to do.

I was disappointed and mad, but I didn't want to judge Adam in any way or get upset. I thought I'd wait for him to tell me what happened. But it was still lousy. To stop me from feeling anything else, I changed into my PJs and went straight to bed.

2

BRAVING ONLINE

In 2015, a little more than a year before being stood up by Adam, I was forty-one and still single, with no kids or pets. Chris and I broke up when I was twenty-seven, and I'd been single since then.

On a sunny weekend morning that summer, I called Rachel for brunch. We decided to meet at Sonsie on Newbury Street. We sat at one of the oval tables facing the open window, looking out at the street, pedestrians, and cars. The sunshine and fresh air felt wonderful. I ordered French toast, one of my go-to favorites, and she ordered salmon benedict. The food didn't take long to arrive. Of course, we both ordered coffee.

"How are you?" she asked affectionately.

"Good. Glad to be back in Boston after having an amazing time in Taiwan." I had been on a two-year hiatus from work to spend time with family, practice yoga, travel, and write. Rachel had experience living outside of Boston and the United States as well.

"Did you make friends there?"

I told her that I did, but she had something more specific in mind. She wanted to know if I'd met any single men. I hadn't.

"What about online dating?" Rachel had met her husband online.

"I tried."

"Not really." A small smile dimpled the corner of her mouth.

At the time, I hadn't really known what I was doing online and had gone out with only a couple of men, which didn't lead anywhere. I couldn't say I'd had a good experience—or any significant online dating experience, for that matter.

Rachel and our mutual friend, Michael, tried before I left on my trip to get me to think about dating and meeting someone online. Michael and I met at my first job. A funny, caring, and worldly brother to me, he had a very cool girlfriend, and we all hung out.

Rachel had brought up the topic of online dating while we all sat on her living room sofa before I left for Taiwan. I had created a profile on OkCupid but hadn't done anything with it.

"You should try it," Rachel said. "It's a good way to meet people."

"Okay," I responded, knowing nothing about online dating.

"Let's take a look now." Michael's enthusiasm permeated the room.

I pulled up the website on her laptop, and the two of them moved closer, one on each side of me. The three of us evaluated profile pictures together.

"What do you think of this one?" Michael asked.

"Hmm. No, not really." I felt embarrassed.

"Why?"

"I don't know." I made a face. I felt uncomfortable and judgmental looking at these profiles. I didn't have words to describe my reactions or be transparent about how I really felt about any particular man's photo.

"How about this one?" Michael moved on to the next person and still wanted to help me find a "like."

My face and ears felt hot. I didn't know how to do this, check men out. I shook my head, but halfway through, I changed my mind and stopped.

Michael decided to click a few "likes" based on what he saw. "Why not?" he said.

"No, no, no! Don't click 'like.'" I grabbed the laptop from him, even though I didn't think about what would or should happen after clicking "like." Clicking on the "like" button seemed like an enormous decision. I was still warming up to the idea of online dating, not prepared to actually proceed. I closed the OkCupid window and let out the tiniest sigh.

Thinking back to what had happened then, I said to Rachel, "Okay. You're right. I didn't really try." She knew me well.

Since that day on the couch, Michael continued to speak favorably about online dating. He'd met his wife online as well. "You're such a catch. Men would love to meet you."

"You are kind to say that." Michael wanted me to find someone and didn't like seeing me alone.

At forty-one, I had no experience dating online. In my twenties and thirties, the single men I met at work or through friends, and who might be interested in me, had all come and gone. Having a relationship had just never been on my mind. Now I didn't know any eligible, single men whom I could meet.

Still, Rachel and Michael repeatedly brought up online dating. After having almost two years of stress-free days in Taipei, I was finally in the right mindset to consider it. I thought about the couples I knew and the husbands in my circle. I wouldn't mind meeting someone like Michael—someone likeminded with goals and similar values in life. The time felt right. *Why not?* I could try it. No harm in seeing what might happen. Mentally, I felt ready to socialize. It was time to start putting in the effort to meet single men.

Unlike the first try, I spent more time carefully constructing my online profile. I opened OkCupid on my computer and followed the steps to recreate an account. I uploaded more recent photos, wrote a short paragraph about myself, and answered questions about me and what I was looking for. I didn't have any technical problems signing up, but I found myself wondering, *How does this work?* I was still embarrassed to look at profiles and judge men I didn't know with a quick yes or no. I didn't want to judge anyone. So I waited. Nothing happened for a few weeks.

"So how's online dating going?" Rachel asked, checking in on me.

"Nothing's happening. I don't think anyone is interested," I said, ready to accept it as a fact.

"Let me take a look at your profile."

I gave Rachel my phone.

"You need better photos," she said.

"What kind?"

"I'll take pictures of you. Let's go out this weekend." I felt silly and excited at the same time.

A few days later, Rachel and I spent a few hours along the Charles River. I sat on a swing, in front of an old tree trunk, and on a park bench while Rachel made me laugh in front of the camera the way only a good friend could. I liked quite a few of the photos she took. Okay, so better photos meant pictures of me doing happy things and laughing. Check.

"What about your profile?" Rachel asked a few days later. "You should write more about yourself and answer more questions. That will help with matching."

I felt comforted being guided by a good friend who had the best intentions and, more importantly, had done what I was trying to do and met with success.

I uploaded the new photos and rewrote my description as if I were speaking to Rachel about myself. It reminded me of something I read once about obituaries: live your life according to how you want your obituary to read. In the case of dating, it worked better to write a bio about myself, of who I thought I was. I wrote more openly about myself, including a description of me reading books, watching movies, and listening to music. The top six things I listed that I could not do without were family and friends, books, my passport, sundresses, oceans, and sushi.

A day later, I started getting messages.

The first person who messaged me was a forty-eight-year-old Jewish man named Ben living in Jamaica Plain and working in finance.

"Nice profile," Ben said first.

"Beautiful picture! Where is it?" I asked, referring to an outdoor photo I saw of him online.

"Arcadia, Maine. Just moved from Brookline. Where do you live?"

"Brookline. Near Star. Where were you in Brookline?" He told me his old street name, and we talked about why he moved from Brookline to Jamaica Plain.

"What are your top three favorite or most memorable places in the world from all your travels? I don't have enough time to go to all the places that interest me. Is Jamaica Plain working out?" I asked.

And just like that, he didn't respond. I didn't know why he stopped sending me messages. I felt awkward. Someone had left me hanging. I thought maybe it was something I said, like I'd switched the topic to focus on him perhaps too quickly. *Maybe I shouldn't have asked him that question. Maybe I should have asked a more casual question. Maybe I shouldn't keep asking questions. What did I do wrong?*

Shortly after embarking on online dating, I wrote regularly to my group of close friends, telling them about each of my dating stories. I was excited about meeting new people and wanted to share my adventures with those who cared about me and hoped for the best. I started consulting with them about my encounters. I didn't have confidence that I knew what I was doing. It made me feel better knowing my friends would protect me from doing stupid things. When I asked, "Was my question too serious too quickly with Ben?" Rachel and Michael both jumped in: "You weren't too serious. Your question wasn't strange. You were just trying to get to know him. He was the one who didn't communicate what he was thinking or feeling. Just move on because he wasn't the one."

Then a man named Carter messaged me, so I read his profile: "First, my profile picture is me with my two adorable nieces, not two women I am courting. Geez, I am not that dumb! Secondly, I am not forty-five. I am fifty-five. 'How dare you?' you might say. Believe it or not, women in my age range usually don't want to go out with me. They say I look too young. I want to show up in the right searches."

I messaged back since I messaged everyone back at the beginning. Again, the conversation didn't last long, and I found myself tracking my steps. Something had been bothering me since the first contact. I didn't feel good about Carter purposely listing a younger age. Was the age a sign I should have noticed early on? Rachel and Michael both told me I didn't have to respond to every single message I received, and Rachel agreed with me, "The age thing is a bit weird."

Connor, thirty-eight, wearing a suit in his profile photo, wrote, "Hi. I hope you had a nice weekend. I think this is the best weather we've had so far this month. I am a nice guy, very stable, but right now I'm really just looking for someone to mess around with on occasion. You are pretty, and I'd like to meet you. If you're interested in giving that a try, send me a message. ;)"

Of course, I didn't respond. Some men just wanted some fun, and that was not what I had in mind. This was a cute, seemingly nice guy's offer—a clear message. I didn't want to be judgmental about this stranger. Perhaps he had a busy schedule. Perhaps he'd just gotten out of a serious and awful relationship. Regardless of the reasons, he was entitled to do what he wanted to do. I gave him points for honesty. At least he was upfront about it.

"OMG, there has to be a better way to say it than 'mess around with,'" Rachel said. "Glad you still have a good sense of humor about dating—definitely the way to go as people are different."

Michael said, "I don't like these guys, honest or not. He's looking for sex with no connection or commitment. That is never what you want. I'm glad you give these guys credit, but it's strange how men seem to have this permission now, while I think women should reject it."

I had a few more message conversations that didn't go anywhere. It always felt like something was not quite right about these guys. I mentioned this to Rachel, and she said, "You can't decide about someone after five minutes of a text conversation. You gotta go out with someone and not just message. Nothing is ever going to happen if you don't meet up." A few days after talking to Rachel, Donny, forty-four and living in Boston, wrote, "Dear Mindy, sorry to hear about the loss of your cat. Where did you grow up, and what do you like doing in your free time?" His headline in his profile sounded interesting: "I am an active, intelligent, kind guy who is looking for someone for a great connection and hopefully a long-term relationship." He had graduated from medical school and was currently in real estate. I liked his first message. He had read my profile and picked up on what I cared about.

"Hi. That's okay. It was a while ago, and Daisy has a good home now. I grew up in Asia and New England. I have a feeling my free time is not packed with as many sporty things as yours. Med school to real estate?" I messaged back.

"True. After being an internist for twelve years, I transitioned into real estate a couple of years ago. The reasons are long and complicated. The short version is that I got hit by the perfect storm of changes in the healthcare system that impacted physicians disproportionately."

"Glad you made the transition that you wanted. Not easy, I am sure. I work at a digital consultancy for healthcare technology. Pretty happy about that. Having success in meeting people here?"

"I am not having success finding people who I want to meet, let alone meeting people here. I suppose that is part of internet dating. Shall we try to meet up and get to know one another face to face sometime next week over drinks?" Donny said.

That was good. I didn't have any concerns. He seemed normal! "Yes, I would like that."

3

I DO NOT

"Why did you and Chris break up?"

Rachel had known me through college, my first job, breakups, more jobs, schizophrenia, and singlehood. Now she was talking about the one important relationship I'd had to this point. She was there when Chris and I started going out and began living together in Back Bay. She and her boyfriend joined us at the movies and dinners, Chris's surprise birthday party, and then the one he threw for me. But over ten years after we broke up, she still didn't understand what actually happened because there were absolutely no warning signs: six years of a seemingly perfect relationship ended abruptly with no drama or any discussion.

In 1996, Chris and I had met when I was a senior at Cornell in Ithaca, New York. We completed the same master's program, so we had the same classes in engineering management. Most of the classes were full of men, and I didn't think of Chris as any different from the others, but he started to talk to me between classes. He was this handsome Asian guy, born in Hong Kong, grew up attending boarding school in Scotland, and ended up in the same place as me for college in the United States. We began doing homework together. Then from homework to dinners to movies. The next thing I knew, summer arrived, and we spent every free minute together. Chris told me later that seeing me with my hair up in a ponytail one day got his attention. I told him his asking me to help him think about his future after graduation nurtured my affection for him. We were young with wide-open eyes, arms, and hearts, and we adored each other. We roamed gorges, hiked forests, played in parks, and hung out in the only small town center nearby. Being a year older, Chris always knew where to go, taking me to quaint restaurants, the one and only mall in the neighborhood, and as many movies as the small cinema played. Without Chris, I lingered on campus in classes, dining halls, and dorms. Cornell and Ithaca felt so much bigger when we were together.

I was attracted to Chris both mentally and physically. He was fit and not lanky like the typical Asian stereotype. He was sporty but not in the American sense with footballs and basketballs. In Scotland, he played and loved rugby. He told me once that football wasn't a real sport like rugby: "We didn't have a whole body of protection." We also both fenced in high school. I loved that commonality about us.

He graduated first, moved to Boston, and began a new life chapter in the corporate world, making new friends, keeping fit, and working hard. I graduated several months later and followed his lead. With his help and planning, I settled in the same city and started working for the same company. Living in the same place again, and without having a conversation about it, we naturally became a couple.

I came to know Chris as loyal, earnest, studious, and occasionally goofy, making funny jokes and faces out of the blue. Career-minded and proud of our accomplishments, we often worked at night and on weekends to make sure we hit our deadlines. We also surrounded ourselves with likeminded friends.

I was deeply moved by how he had taken care of me when I found a benign cyst in my left breast. He always knew what to do: what medication to get, where to get food, and who to call. Chris's spontaneous tenderness touched me; I felt loved and thankful to have him by my side.

In some ways, we were both children at heart. Some of our favorite movies were the Disney ones. He owned almost every one. We accommodated our different tastes in film as well. He preferred action and sci-fi movies, while I loved sappy romantic comedies. Regardless, we watched everything together. At first, we were both flexible in nature and considerate of the other person's preferences, alternating who chose the restaurant for dinner or picked which movie to watch. We were comfortable with each other and had similar temperaments. I could tell Chris everything on my mind. We took care of each other in our own ways. We spent every minute together outside of work. Those first few years were happy ones.

Slowly, there was a shift in the balance between the two of us. I started to defer to Chris, and he eventually became in charge of our lives.

Chris often turned to me after we both got into his car after work. "What do you want to eat for dinner?"

"I'm okay with anything. What do you feel like having?"

"Let's go for Thai food. Brown Sugar."

"Sounds good to me." I easily acquiesced and began doing it willingly when it came to food, movies, video games, shopping, golfing, or how we spent our leisure time.

"Let's take a vacation," Chris said one day, about a year into our relationship. I'd never taken a vacation as an adult. Chris knew how to enjoy life better than I did.

"Okay."

"Let's go on a cruise."

I smiled wide. That sounded good to me.

In January, Chris booked everything for us. He picked the airline and the cruise line. We packed our bags and flew to Miami. We took a taxi to the seaport and boarded an enormous Carnival *Imagination* ship. Our room on the lower deck, one of the smallest, had no windows. We put down our bags and went to the upper deck to watch the ship leave Miami.

The sun shone against the bright blue sky—not a single cloud. We found a spot on the deck that we liked and spent a few hours soaking in the sun. Chris read his book, while I napped. After a few hours, we explored the rest of the ship.

I stood on the top deck of the ship, gazing at how the sky blended with the blue water. Such complete openness amazed me. The view was nothing like Boston, where high-rises blocked the sky and cars and people crowded the streets. We had completely disconnected from our normal lives— no internet and utter peace. I closed my eyes and tried to memorize the stunning view. I opened my eyes to make sure I'd remembered correctly. I closed my eyes again, imagining the blueness, and counted from one to ten. I wanted to forever be able to recall what I saw.

The brilliant sun and azure sky lasted for the next few days. We alternated spending time at sea and on land in the Caribbean, Grand Cayman, and Tulum, Mexico.

Toward the end of our trip, I discovered a spa on the ship. "Should I get a massage? I've never had one." I wondered how it would feel. I looked at all the different massages on the menu. "It's expensive."

"Try it if you want. You can afford it," Chris encouraged me. Having already paid for the trip, he wanted me to be as comfortable as he was in spending money on one's self. He was used to such a mindset, which was different from how I'd grown up. I never had extra money. I spent my free time with books at home if I was not babysitting. A night out at the local movie theater—a twelve-dollar ticket—was a big deal and enjoyment for me. Now that I had a decent job, I felt I already spent a lot more money on food and clothes. Chris didn't have the same hesitation I had with money. He was smart about it. He was also more adventurous when it came to trying new things, even though we were both generous in nature.

"Why not? I am going to try it."

A woman greeted me in the waiting area, showed me the locker room, and explained what I needed to do to get ready. A few minutes later, a second woman introduced herself as the masseuse and led me to a darker room with a bed in the middle. She stepped out and was back in a few minutes. "May I come in?" The scent of lavender permeated the room. Calming music played in the background.

I felt her hands on my back, releasing all the stress from nonstop typing in front of a computer. Then she worked on my arms and legs. I felt my muscles relaxing. *My body works hard. This is amazing.* It felt so luxurious.

Chris waited for me in the library, where I met him after I finished.

"How was it?" he asked.

"I loved it—totally worth it."

"Great!"

After four blissful days, we returned to Miami and debarked from *Imagination*. Once on land, I turned and looked at the enormous ship. My body kept moving slightly to the left and right as if there were still waves around me. "Wow, I still have my sea legs." I laughed, hoping I would soon adjust to being on land.

"Good trip?" Chris put his arm around me.

"Amazing!" I closed my eyes and saw the blueness of the open space in my mind. I opened my eyes and looked at Chris. Then we both smiled. At that moment, I felt my life experience was tied to Chris's, and because of him, I had a better life. I felt loved, safe, and content.

Seven months after the cruise, Chris's twenty-seventh birthday was coming up. In the past, I'd gotten him nice gifts like a watch, an expensive sweater, or an unusual silk tie. But this time, I wanted to do something different: throw him a surprise birthday party. I could easily enlist Rachel and her boyfriend, who lived downstairs. They had a spare key to our apartment and could sneak in without any problem. A week before the party, I emailed our friends and told everyone the specific time to be there. Rachel would let everyone in.

On the morning of the party, Chris wanted to go shopping and walk around Copley Place and Prudential Mall. I knew he liked going out on weekends and that I'd have no problem getting him to leave the apartment. We walked around the mall for a while. At the appropriate time, I asked Chris if he wanted to buy anything.

"Not really," he said.

"Want to head home?"

"Sure."

My heart started racing. He parked the car in the back of

the building. I didn't want to talk and hoped Chris wouldn't try to start a conversation because my voice might break from the excitement. We made our way from the basement's back door to the second floor and our apartment. I followed him instead of going first. He took out his key and opened the front door.

"Surprise!" everyone in the apartment shouted.

Chris heard the loud sound and instinctively ducked. I saw his knees hit the wood floor with a loud thump. His face became very red. He looked around and saw all the familiar faces. Everyone was laughing and wishing him a happy birthday. He took a few seconds to collect himself, stood up, picked up his cat, and sat down on the sofa.

I went over to him. "Are you surprised?"

He was absolutely in shock. "I thought there was a burglar in the apartment." His face had turned red, but he smiled at me. He patted himself on the chest, still hugging his cat. Although happy the surprise had worked so well, I worried about his reaction. Had I overdone it? Maybe I should've planned the surprise in a public place and not at home.

Chris stopped patting his chest, let go of the cat, and started socializing with our friends. I kept watching him and breathed a sigh of relief. At the end of the night, it felt like the party was a great success. All our friends were with us to celebrate Chris on his special day.

For my birthdays, Chris gave me adorable stuffed animals. I always happily thanked him. Like not having extra money, I also didn't grow up with stuffed animals as a kid. If I remember correctly, I had one: a Snoopy. Chris had a few of his own favorites at home. I believe they were gifts from his parents and ex-girlfriends. Not only did he like receiving them, but he loved giving them as gifts. Over the years, he had given me Gund bears and Pooh bears. I had them lined up on a bookshelf in the living room, while he preferred his on the guest bed.

Michael heard about the gift and told me his girlfriend would have killed him if he'd given her a stuffed animal. I thought that was an odd thing to say. Every year, the stuffed animals from Chris got bigger and bigger. On my birthday, three months after his surprise party, I got the largest Patrick the Pup plush dog from FAO Schwartz in New York City. Patrick was so big that he took up a seat on our sofa. I'd never thought about what I wanted or even if I liked stuffed animals. To be fair, Chris also introduced me to Tiffany's. I still have the matching ring, bracelet, and necklace that he gave me from the Tiffany Elsa Peretti Bean Collection. I loved getting whatever Chris gave me.

One night, five years into our relationship, three couples met us at a restaurant for dinner. I arrived last. I was excited to see all my friends. I hugged them and started chatting, completely forgetting to say hello to Chris, who sat in the corner. It was only until I sat down that I noticed him. Later on, on other occasions, I noticed couple after couple meeting at restaurants or bars, saying hello to each other first, perhaps with a soft kiss, and then saying hi to everyone else. Was Chris becoming less important to me?

On rare occasions, Chris openly disagreed with me. One winter, which, unbeknownst to me at the time, was near the end of our relationship, we started making arrangements for the holidays. I planned to visit my parents for Thanksgiving. "Do you want to come with me to visit my parents?"

He didn't even hesitate. "No, not really." I originally

thought Chris might have just been shy, because I'd met his parents and sisters a while before. I'd even joined his family on a trip to Barcelona; they included me in everything they did. I'd also been to his parents' home in Vancouver and had been very happy to meet his family. Why was Chris not interested in meeting my parents at all? Was it important to me if he did or didn't meet them? Did I just naturally expect him to reciprocate? I didn't realize that my relationship with Chris revolved around him and his world.

Clearly, there were hints here and there that our relationship may not have been heading to a good place, but I didn't pick up on any of the clues until Chris and I slept in one Sunday morning. I was under the covers and had just woken up; our backs were to each other with a space in the middle of the bed between us that felt like an enormous chasm. I opened and closed my eyes as a wave of strong emotion washed over me, but I didn't dare move. I felt no love from the person sleeping next to me. There I was with Chris right beside me, but I felt lonely at a time when I least expected to.

"How do you think we're doing?" I asked Chris that day. I held a cup of tea and sat on the living room sofa, while he was at the dining table adjacent to the room I was in. I'd never had a relationship conversation with Chris during our entire six years together, so this was a first.

Chris didn't even look up from his laptop when he spoke to me. "If you're thinking of marriage, I don't want to get married right now."

I immediately remembered the story about a female acquaintance of ours who stayed in a relationship for years and even bought a house with her boyfriend. Ten years later, he broke up with her and married another woman a year after. When Chris said he didn't want to get married right then, I understood he didn't want to marry *me*.

My heart sank. My body went stiff. Silence filled the room. The sunlight shone through the bay window in the living room, hurting my eyes. I felt rejected but straightened my back, trying to sit up taller. I didn't look at Chris. Instead, I looked out the window.

"I think I should move out." My shield went up, and I protected myself instinctually.

"You sure?" He didn't sound upset. It was as if I'd just asked where we should have dinner or what movie we should watch—as if this were just a routine conversation.

"Yes, I think I should." I decided on the spot. *Let's break up while we're still speaking to each other. I'm not waiting for ten years to become a bitter woman who hates you.*

"Okay." He went back to his computer.

This conversation didn't make me turn on Chris. Instead, I finally started asking myself, *Who am I? What kind of person do I want to be? What kind of life do I want to have?* I realized that I needed to walk away from Chris to find myself. There was no hostility between us at all. From me, it was simple acceptance. Since we didn't talk about it, I don't know what Chris thought of it. Perhaps he thought we were just taking a short break and we could get back together. However, he didn't argue with me or try to get me back in the weeks and months that followed. The spark between us was long gone, even though the support for each other was still there. Perhaps we were already just friends. Even though we continued to spend time together after this, mostly initiated by Chris, the change—the breakup—was cemented in my mind. Just like how we became a couple naturally without any discussion, we became just friends overnight after this short exchange.

4

A PLACE TO SLEEP

The first few years after I moved out of Chris's apartment in Back Bay, I struggled with setting up my own place. I'd never thought about what kind of home I wanted for myself since I'd moved into Chris's place soon after graduating from college. Rachel offered to search for a new home with me, realizing how difficult it would be for me to look for such a thing by myself. I was thankful to have someone with me on the search even though I hadn't thought to ask for help. I just knew I needed to find a place.

I'd heard about Brookline being a great place to live, so I decided to look there. Brookline was a little bit outside and west of Boston. A woman met Rachel and me at a place I'd found: a small, one-bedroom apartment on the ground floor in the back of a brick apartment building near Coolidge Corner.

"I'm from Russia. Where are you from?" a tall woman with a stocky frame said with a heavy accent. My rental application on the kitchen counter listed Chris's place as my current address and Rachel as a personal reference.

"I'm from Taiwan but came to the United States as a teenager. Everything looks new here."

"We lived here while we did the renovation ourselves. My husband, me, and my son," she said.

"How were you able to do that?" I looked around the six-hundred-square-foot space, trying to imagine three adults living there.

"We moved the furniture to one side of the room and worked on the other side. I want to sell this place for good money. It's been on the market for a few months with no one buying. So I thought I'd rent it out for now. Just you? Do you have pets?" She looked me up and down as if to see if I was the type to throw wild parties.

"Just me. No pets."

"Good. The monthly rent is one hundred and forty-five dollars, heat and hot water included. Electricity and gas are not. No phone. I am offering a six-month lease."

"Would you give us a few minutes?" I asked. She nodded and stepped to the side.

I turned to Rachel. "What do you think?" I whispered. "I like this place."

"It's nice, and the rent is fair. But don't you want to look at other places? And what about it only being for six months?"

"I'm okay with that because it gives me the option to move if I don't like living here. Let me just take it."

"Cool," Rachel said.

I walked back to the landlord. "I'll take it." I signed the lease the next day and paid a deposit and the first month's rent. In addition to a standard rental lease agreement, she also asked me to sign an apartment condition statement, which said, "We have examined the premises and have found the present condition to be as follows: property in acceptable condition with no defects or conditions requiring repairs."

A couple of weeks later, on November 1, Chris helped me move into my new place. To me, Chris was still a dear person in my life. When I needed help, he showed up. It may not have been understandable to our friends, but it was completely acceptable and reasonable to Chris and me. He helped me move out of his place, rented a U-Haul, and lifted all the heavy boxes. "Your place looks nice," he said when seeing it for the first time.

Once I started looking for my own home, it hit me that I had no furniture of my own. I had to buy everything and do it in a hurry. I wanted a nice bed and devoted the most time to that. I ordered a wooden bed frame from Pottery Barn and bought the same Beautyrest mattress that Chris had because I knew I liked it. For the rest, I went to nearby Pier One and bought everything I needed, cobbling together what I could from that one store. Comfort wasn't a priority—I just wanted to get it done.

After I moved in, my home felt so quiet. *Too* quiet and cold. Not in the habit of cooking for myself, I rarely used the kitchen, and eating out was easy. The new fridge stayed empty. Watching TV had been Chris's thing, so I didn't buy a television. I spent my time reading on an uncomfortable beige Papasan chair from Pier One that had looked good but was better for collecting dust. I couldn't enjoy tea because I hadn't bought any teabags. I didn't bother with window treatments. I never used the locked back door, which led to an unlit parking lot. My home was mostly a place for me to shower in and sleep.

On a Friday night after a date with Chris—we were in an on-again/off-again stage—he dropped me off at my place and noticed the light on in the living room. Chris told me to stay at the entrance. He went inside to see if anyone was still in my apartment. Then I saw the open window in the living room facing the parking lot. Someone had broken in! Thank goodness I wasn't home when it had happened. I'd hoped they hadn't stolen my passport.

Chris came back to me. "You can come in. No one is here."

I walked around my small apartment. Someone had dumped the stuff that was in several organized boxes—mostly paper—onto my bed. My jewelry box had been emptied out. Its contents weren't expensive but had sentimental value. My laptop and digital camera were gone. I didn't have anything else worth taking.

Chris called 911. A Brookline policewoman and her partner came in less than five minutes. She looked around and told me to file a report.

"Do you live here alone?" the policewoman asked while her colleague stayed outside in the parking lot, visible from my window.

"Yes. It's just me. The light was on, and the window was open when I came home."

"Let me take a look at the back." She leaned outside of the window with a flashlight and talked to the other policeman. The lock on the backdoor had remained untouched, but the window had been forced open. She checked out my bedroom next.

"How likely is it that you will catch this person or find my lost items?" I asked.

"We can look for fingerprints. Maybe around the window. Or this. Can I take this empty jewelry box? Maybe we can get clear prints off this." Meanwhile, the policeman dusted the window frame outside.

"Yes, please take it." She lifted my wooden box with a gloved hand and placed it into a plastic bag. "It's unlikely we'll catch someone for break-ins like this. You can file a report listing all your lost items. Be descriptive. We might see them elsewhere." After about thirty minutes, she said, "I'm afraid there's nothing more we can do at this point. If you see anyone suspicious, call 911 again."

After Chris and the police left, I felt unsafe. I should have avoided a ground-level apartment with a door and a window facing a dark parking lot. No wonder someone broke in. I spent the night and the rest of that weekend remembering, listing, and drawing my lost jewelry on paper, which I then submitted to the police. I didn't care about the cheap items I'd bought in college, but there were three or four pieces from recent trips that I really missed. Luckily, I was wearing the Tiffany Bean collection that Chris gave me, the only surviving jewelry from the break-in.

I notified my landlady, who rushed over the next day. She wanted to know if the apartment was damaged in any way. She changed the lock on the backdoor.

A little while later, she sent a letter letting me know she would not extend the lease beyond six months and that she'd appreciate it if I moved out on time. I got the sense that she was protective of her apartment and wanted to make sure it stayed in good shape so she could sell it for a good price or rent it out again. It felt like being kicked out. So I began looking for a new place.

At this point, I felt unsafe and believed I should not live alone. When my friend John from work told me he needed a new housemate, I immediately said, "When can I move in?"

John's house had three floors. On the first floor, there was a garage and one bedroom with a small bathroom. The living room, dining area, and kitchen were on the second floor. Two more bedrooms and a bathroom were on the third floor. With Chris and John's help, I quickly moved into one of the bedrooms on the top floor in his house in East Cambridge. Except for keeping what fit in my new bedroom, I had to give away all of the other furniture I had purchased six months before since John's house had stuff packed in all the common areas. I still had given no real thought to what I needed or wanted in a home.

John's house proved to be even more isolating than my Brookline place. I spent my life going between my office near Cambridge Galleria Mall and my new home a few blocks away, with nothing else within walking distance.

Given that there were no restaurants or grocery stores within walking distance between work and home, I had to go out of my way to get food. I decided to get a membership with Zipcar to rent a car quickly and drive to the closest grocery store. I never got comfortable with that and still preferred taking the T into Boston to eat out on weekends when I had the time. The kitchen also didn't feel like mine. I didn't know what cookware and gadgets were there, not wanting to go through other people's things.

I also hadn't thought it through that I hadn't lived with roommates since my first and second years in college. One day, I came home and went upstairs to the second-floor living room and then up one more floor to my bedroom. As I turned from the stairs to my space, I saw a person standing in the middle of my bedroom. It was my other housemate. *What is she doing in my room?* I felt violated. "Hi," I said.

"Oh, you're home. You said I could borrow your books."

"True," I said, still feeling uneasy.

"Okay, I'd better go." She walked out of my room. I quickly and quietly closed the door behind her.

My uneasiness and discomfort continued. How could someone I didn't know well feel entitled to go into my private living space? I ended up retreating to my own room most of the time and not lingering in the common area. That's when something started going wrong.

5

A RUNAWAY MIND

I noticed my surrounding more because I had more time being alone. I was horrible at being on my own. I started hearing and seeing things I couldn't understand. I thought everything had meanings. A hand rubbing a nose. (Someone was sending me a sign!) *Think about it.* A loud bang from slamming a door shut. (Another sign!) *Don't do that.* A car starting its engine on the side of a street. (A coded message again!) *You're on the right track.* When I listened to music on an iPod, I started noticing certain phrases. *Is someone talking to me through the song?* As I read books, I heard tiny clicking sounds as I read certain words. *Is someone sending me a coded message: "come, next, here"?* At the gym, I saw the treadmill room filled with women running in place except for one empty machine. I believed the women all planned to be there to cheer me on after my tough day at work. I almost cried before I started. *I feel supported. Should I?*

One weekend, I wandered the city on the T, not sure where to get off, and saw the whole train empty out at Park Street. *Everyone is getting off here. Is something going on? Are they telling me to get off?* Recently finding that roommate in my room made me wonder what else she might be doing when I wasn't there. I read meaning into many things. Alone, there was no one to tell me I was making something out of nothing. Slowly, what I saw as "magical moments" increased. I became timid and shier than usual. I felt anxious every time a "special moment" occurred and became hypersensitive to everything I experienced from the outside world. Tiny sounds or gestures alerted me every few days, then every few hours, then every few minutes. In some odd way, it felt fun, and I didn't think anything was wrong with me.

As I continued living a life alone, filled with delusional thoughts, I started hearing a voice talking to me: the deciding symptom of schizophrenia.

I stood in front of my house door and locked it, ready for work.

"Can you hear me?"

"Yes," I said quietly and smiled. *What is this, and who is this?* Whoever it was sounded gentle. I pictured a young man my age. The voice rang very clearly in a calm, sweet tone as if a real person spoke. I looked around the street and saw no one else there.

"Don't smile. You're going to look silly if you walk down the street, talk to yourself, and smile on your own."

Okay.

"You need to ask someone for help," the voice said.

Jennifer? I thought immediately.

"No, it has to be a single guy."

Is this some sort of joke?

"No, this is not a joke. This is serious," the voice said.

When I arrived at work—about a ten-minute walk from home—he disappeared. I thought nothing of it and forgot the whole experience shortly afterward.

A few days later, I heard him again. I faced him mostly on my own, though I had mentioned him to Chris, Rachel, and Michael. My friends didn't know how to help me. While I worked normally during the day at a software product company as a software configuration engineer, more and more anxiety steadily built up in my brain over a few months. Every few minutes, I noticed something around me that seemed strange. Someone walked in a circle in front of my cubicle. *Checking on me?* Someone came to ask me a question about a message I just sent him. *How did he know so fast? Can someone see my screen?* I went to the bathroom, and someone blocked the door. *Is he doing that on purpose? Does he know I need to go?*

The tipping point came when I heard nonstop talking for a couple of days and couldn't sleep. "Keep it up," he said as I tried to read. "Really?" as I changed into my PJs. The one voice commented on everything I did. My mind was so worked up that I became catatonic that weekend. I called Chris for help in the middle of the night. He picked me up and took me to his place. I was completely out of it. He took me to see a psychiatrist as soon as he could on Monday. I don't remember much about what happened at his place or during my first doctor's appointment. At age thirty, I had triggered schizophrenia and started taking medication. Chris hoped the medication would end my symptoms. After staying with him over the weekend and on Monday, I went home and continued with my single life.

Taking Zyprexa was immediately effective and completely

cleared any auditory hallucinations. However, after that psychotic episode, my thinking was still not corrected. I held on to those fragmented memories from my first psychotic episode. I remembered so clearly the young man's voice created by my brain. *I'll call you Joe.* My mind went back to him often, especially when I was alone, sometimes for a few minutes on a bus ride, during a walk, or before I went to bed. I'd felt curious and magical when I'd first heard from him.

During my thirties, the following eight years after meeting Joe, schizophrenia became a significant force in my private life.

I was not equipped to manage my schizophrenia because I was not fully aware of what was going on inside my brain. I felt like my life had been pretty normal and ordinary up to that point.

What I experienced was illogical, so I tried to combat it with logic. Unfortunately, using logic to fight something that's illogical and mysterious didn't work. But there was no one there to help me walk out of this maze. Alone, I kept circling around the same thoughts again and again. Yet I discussed my breakdown with no one, not even with my doctor.

Life just went back to before, but after having had the mental breakdown in East Cambridge, I didn't want to live there anymore because it reminded me of all the voices and sounds I'd heard there. I'd only lived there a little more than a year. Then it was time to move again.

In April 2004, a couple of months after that breakdown, I decided to buy my own apartment. Many of my friends owned their places, and I thought it was a good idea for me too. Since I'd always had a decent job, I had enough savings for a down payment. I calculated a monthly payment I could afford and came up with a price range for an apartment. Luckily, I found a reasonably priced one-bedroom apartment in Back Bay, one of my favorite neighborhoods. I'd be close to shops and restaurants as well as public transportation, which was perfect for me.

On the closing day, my hands didn't tremble. No tears running down my cheeks. No racing heart thumping inside my chest. I was satisfied with my largest purchase in life. I didn't look for a perfect place but one that was perfect for me. It was in good condition, and I didn't have to do any renovation. I couldn't wait to get settled in this seven-hundred-square-foot space. Somehow, I thought of Chris for the first time in a while. *This is why Chris and I are just friends—so that I can buy my own place.* In fact, I felt that we were great friends. I knew that if I needed his help, all I had to do was call, and he would show up. Then the thought disappeared as quickly as it came.

On a beautiful summer day, I wandered around on Newbury Street and walked home in minutes. No need to hop on the T to go home from a bookstore that I'd just visited. Everything was only blocks away. It suited me well.

A few months after moving in and visiting a friend's place, I came home feeling something amiss. *It doesn't feel lived in.* During my first few months as a homeowner, I added new furniture—a sofa, dining table, and dining chairs. The place looked very functional. The yellow sofa matched the soft-yellow painted wall. Books on topics I loved filled my bookshelf in the long hallway. My place, however, lacked accent pieces; it needed more character. As much as I desired a simple and neat home, I also needed to make it mine. Over the next twelve months, I added pictures to the bare walls, a basket for magazines, reading lamps, and a clock. I thought about creating my own paintings, but Rachel and Michael kindly discouraged me, telling me to simply buy a few pieces. *I know. I know. I'm never going to finish a painting. And it wouldn't look so good either, but it is fun to think about it.* Owning a place made no difference in my spending habits. Now instead of paying someone rent, I paid myself and the bank. It was the biggest loan I'd ever taken out. I learned about interest rates, principal versus interest payments, condominium fees, and city taxes.

The T stop closest to my apartment was the Hynes Convention Center stop on the green line. Sometimes a homeless person slept in the small nook of the exit off Newbury Street. Seeing homeless individuals made me feel extremely thankful for how far I'd come in my life. I'd done so much for myself, but I was also lucky to be supported by family and friends. One special day, soon after I bought the apartment, my dad sent me a letter. Dad had been the most important anchor for me in life. In the envelope, there was one single sheet of paper with a handwritten note: "Dear Mindy, congratulations. I'll bring my toolbox. Love, Dad."

6

GOING SOLO

At twenty-seven, without a boyfriend, being alone meant having to learn how to spend time with myself. I wanted to make a better connection with my inner thoughts and desires, to become a stronger person, especially after all I'd been through. I wanted to grow more as a person and do more. I believed that through reading and running, I could become both mentally and physically stronger. I started running and going to the gym for the first time in my life. It took some trying, but in the middle of the summer, I could run the three-mile loop along the Charles River between Longfellow Bridge and Harvard Bridge. I felt great.

I realized I loved exploring Boston on foot. Chris never wanted to walk anywhere because he preferred the convenience of driving to places. After spending some time at Trident Booksellers and Café and other brunch places in Back Bay, I took walks along the Charles River. I loved to walk during my free time. During the summer in Boston, more locals filled the sidewalks, enjoying the beautiful, warm weather. With out-of-town college students back home, every place was less congested, with one exception: the beloved Charles River beach.

The morning crowd showed up to sunbathe along the river with full gear, including beach chairs, books, snacks, and blankets. Around lunchtime, accidental drop-ins appeared in their casual-best outfits, filling up all the benches, hoping to avoid dirtying their clothes. Late risers showed up fashionably late in proper beachwear and filled the air with the smell of sunblock. Just when the sun began to set, families and dog walkers packed the rest of the empty spaces. Besides jumping into the water and building sandcastles, people enjoyed the sun, the beach, and novice sailors out in the river. After living in Boston for six years, I finally got to know the city the way I wanted to.

One day, I saw an advertisement for a movie I wanted to see. *Why not just go?* The closest theater at the time was located in Copley Place. I walked to the theater feeling adventurous. I bought one ticket and went inside. As I stood in the entryway, anxiety rose inside me. I didn't know where to sit, although the place was pretty empty. It felt huge, and I felt small. I picked a corner seat to the side and sat down. I fussed with my hands, not sure where to put them. I became very aware of being alone. This was before we all had smartphones that could connect us to friends, the internet, or even 911 in seconds. I didn't know what to do with myself. But I figured it out. I calmed myself. I put my hands in my lap and settled down into the seat. I made myself comfortable. I waited for the movie to start. My brain relaxed and went blank. I was mindful of that quiet moment. Then the movie started, and from there I was okay. This was huge: learning how to go to the movies by myself and understanding that I could be comfortable all alone. How empowering: I could go ahead and do whatever I wanted to all by myself.

Eating out solo offered another kind of adventure. I liked trying different cuisines, and since I didn't have someone to go with me readily, I decided to start having solo dates with myself.

The first time I ate alone was at Trident Booksellers and Café on Newbury Street. It was on a weekend morning when I craved brunch food. I saw an empty bar seat and asked about it. The bar seats were first come, first served. No waiting list. I sat down and saw other singles around me, thus starting my love affair with bar seats. People in groups didn't generally sit there, so for singles like me, they were great. I got the same menu as everyone else in the restaurant. The bartenders understood and appreciated single customers. They were welcoming but at the same time respectful of personal space. If I wanted to chat, they'd chat. If I preferred quiet, they let me be. As a bonus, I skipped the long waits reserved for customers who wanted to sit at a table.

I started spending more time at Trident on weekends. I'd order waffles or French toast and coffee while reading my Kindle or writing on my laptop. I became very comfortable and felt peaceful among all the diners and book shoppers. This was my routine for years. I recognized many waiters and waitresses and vice versa. Sometimes I even had the courage to strike up a conversation with strangers—something Chris and I together never would have done. One waitress at Trident, Jane, knew my standard order well and often made fun of me for asking for the menu every single time.

Dinners, however, were trickier because I didn't think it was appropriate to read or write while eating at that time. Dinner was a formal event to me, and I didn't want to be impolite. Again, this was before we had smartphones. I remember walking into a restaurant and asking for a table for one. That in itself felt awkward at first. Similar to my first time alone at a movie theater, I didn't know what to do with my body. I fidgeted while reading the menu. I skipped a few lines as I looked through what was in front of me. I hurried even though the waiter was completely fine with me taking my time. I limited my selection to one or two dishes since there was no one with whom to share the meal. It took a few more tries before I realized that ordering more meant I had some yummy leftovers for the next day at home. I swore away my personal rule of no leftovers, never having had the habit to eat at home, and always ended up throwing away leftovers that went bad eventually.

Eating solo also meant no talking during the meal. While waiting for the food to come, I people-watched or spaced out—a good time to take a mental break. Once the food came, my focus was completely on my meal: looking at it, cutting, picking, and chewing it. I learned to enjoy my food this way. I made myself slow down and stopped swallowing big bites quickly as if I had somewhere urgent to run to. Eating became a hobby. Sometimes I made reservations at high-ranking restaurants; other times I just wandered into a hole in the wall serendipitously. Boston was a great place to be a solo foodie. There were endless possibilities—from Japanese, Thai, and Ethiopian to Vietnamese, Mediterranean, and Sicilian. I tried and loved them all.

When my twenty-eighth birthday came around, four girl-friends from work invited me to a special birthday lunch. After we ate at Cheesecake Factory, each friend held out a small surprise gift for me. Each gift had a special message.

A heavenly scented lavender soap had a note that said,

"Pamper yourself, treat yourself well, and you will be surrounded by people who treat you well. Love, T."

A rainbow-colored set of Post-it pads read, "Today is a happy time / Write it down on a Post-it / To highlight the memory / Stick it where you'll see it / As a happy reminder / When a day is not so happy.—J."

A music-sheet paperweight said, "When you feel the weight of the world upon your shoulders, sing a little song . . . do a little dance. From, Y."

A huge white sandalwood-scented candle had a note attached saying, "There is always a light at the end of any tunnel; it's just a matter of finding it. So when things are the darkest, don't despair, because your light may be around the next bend. Love, S."

The emptiness left by Chris's absence had slowly filled with friendship. I reconnected with old friends and made new ones. Living as a single person didn't mean being alone all the time. After the breakup, when I lost touch and routines with our "couple" friends, I luckily didn't stay alone for long. Quite the opposite: I started to be even more social than I'd been with Chris.

First, I met many people at work from both my first and second jobs; we became close friends over time. From my first job, my old couple friends and I recalibrated our friendship with my being single, while many of them had gotten married. At my second job, I learned once again how to meet new people and carry on interesting social conversations. Someone at the office always had an idea for what we should do on a Thursday or Friday night. With married friends, I went to fancy restaurants to get away from the daily grind. With single friends, karaoke bars and nightclubs helped us destress from the week.

Other singles met people, while I tucked myself in the back of the group, sipping the drink of the day. We often had beers with dinner. I loved the live bands playing acoustic music. I didn't sing, but I danced. I loved just being with friends.

Even when some of my friends got married, we continued spending time with each other. I made sure to reach out to Rachel and Michael regularly. We all made keeping in touch a priority. I am lucky to have had such a social life.

7

FOG MEETINGS

During dinner conversations with Rachel and Michael, when I'd been on my own for a year or so, the topic of Chris occasionally came up.

"How's he doing?" Rachel gave me a pointed look. Rachel and Michael had been friends with him when Chris and I were together. Even though we'd broken up, friends still asked me about him because they knew we still got together from time to time. I guessed I wasn't the only one having trouble adjusting to the end of a six-year habit. I believed we were friends, and so did he.

"He's fine. Doing an MBA and trying to change his career." And, yes, I was still cat-sitting for him when he went out of town. "I think he's seeing some girl he met at school." I had just hung out with them a few weeks ago. Chris still called me for dinners or movies from time to time, and I'd never said no to his invitation. I'd met several of his female friends, though I was never quite sure what their status was, and I never asked. Knowing Chris, I was sure that they didn't talk about it.

After Chris, men were not on my mind at all. I went through the mechanics of talking about dating when Rachel mentioned it. Getting another boyfriend was not a priority, although I didn't purposely try to stay single.

One day, out of the blue, Rachel—who was single at the time—asked me if I wanted to check out FirstFriday, a social event held at the Museum of Fine Arts on the first Friday of every month. She thought we could meet people there. I was curious enough to say yes, so we went together.

We paid the admission fee as if we were there to admire the artwork, except we were there to admire a different kind of artwork: men. Tall and short. Slim and built. I preferred crewcuts over long and wavy hair. I admired men who took the time to dress in modern and sophisticated attire. Most importantly, I was attracted to men who expressed friendliness and made me feel welcome.

The space we were directed to was a pleasant room filled with European Renaissance paintings. Three musicians in one corner of the room played jazz and created a congenial mood.

Rachel and I started talking about dating: the nightmares and the joys. "Have you been to FirstFriday before?" I asked her.

"Yes, I came once with another friend."

"Did you meet anyone?"

"No, but at least we're out."

"There seems to be a wide range of eclectic men here. All ages. How is dating life for you?" I looked around.

"Nothing's happening. I already know all the single guys in my community. Now I have to branch out. I don't know if I'm being too picky."

"Well, you have to like the guy to be with him forever. I've never met someone this way. It feels so random to me," I confessed.

Initially, we were both antisocial and kept mostly to ourselves.

"I have a rule for myself. We have to individually approach three men," Rachel said, reminding both of us why we were there. "Anyone look interesting to you?"

"I'm up for the challenge. The guy over there with the orange sweater. He's standing in a circle with those women, dancing." Slim. Stylish. Smiling. Good-looking.

"He looks interesting. But he's also surrounded by a group of women already. Let's find someone else who's alone. Might be easier," Rachel recommended.

I realized that all the women there were probably after the same few men. I didn't want to be competitive and be just one more woman involved in the chase. I didn't see anyone else who looked worth approaching.

A couple in front of us affectionately kissed, with their hands moving all over each other. I guessed some people were having a good time, but we didn't need to watch that. "Let's move to a different spot," I suggested. Rachel agreed.

We ended up standing in a hidden corner on the side watching men walk by. We grabbed some snacks when waiters with trays came our way. Occasionally, we pointed out someone good-looking.

Finally, a man around our age made an effort to interrupt us and strike up a conversation. He sported a mustache and wore a beret, both a turnoff for me. His out-of-proportion face looked unwieldy.

"Hi. I'm Ian. How are you?"

"I'm Rachel, and this is Mindy. You enjoying the night?"

"Great music. Nice art. Do you know these paintings?"

"Not really, but they're great," Rachel said. I kept quiet. I knew that neither she nor I felt any connection. He walked away after a long silence among us.

"That was awkward," I said to Rachel.

"We're not having a lot of luck. He wasn't my type really. By the way, we're not doing well as far as our three-men target goes." We both laughed.

The night went by fast actually. I had a great time talking to Rachel. That was all I cared about at the time with this social experience. Whatever I do, I enjoy doing it with good friends. Besides that, I didn't find this event suitable or interesting enough for me to go back.

When I spent time with Rachel and Michael, they liked meeting new people. For me, it was about hanging out with them. The funny thing is that I had no trouble being social, talkative, friendly, and outgoing at work or with friends and family, but as soon as I met a man who was single and attractive to me, I became a complete introvert. My change of personality surprised both me and my friends since they knew me as easygoing, friendly, and sociable. I was rusty when it came to meeting and dating men.

The first time I went out with a single man after my relationship with Chris happened shortly after the breakup. Seth, who'd worked with me at my first job, decided to ask me out. Great—a couple of years older, smart, kind, and recently single: my type of man. He suggested we go to the Isabella Stewart Gardner Museum, where I'd never been. He paid for our tickets, and we walked around for several hours, not holding hands and not saying much. I wondered if he noticed the difference between how I acted at work and how I responded to him at the museum. At work, I was social and communicative. When our date ended and he said he had a good time, I quickly said goodbye and rushed away.

Dan was the first person who made a strong impression on me after Chris. We met at work when I started my second job at age twenty-nine. I had a crush on him, so whenever I saw him, I felt timid and anxious. Even though we ran into each other because we worked and worked out at the same places, we never had a proper conversation. In addition to work and our local gym, I ran into him on the T due to the proximity of where we lived.

One time, a group of us from work went to a happy hour at an Irish bar in the North End. I sat in a corner and enjoyed listening to and watching everyone. After most of the group left, Dan asked me if I wanted to hang out. "Sure," I said.

We got up from our corner and stood next to each other at the bar. Dan watched the basketball game on the TV above us. I didn't know any sports teams, and I rarely hung out at bars. We said nothing to each other for the next half hour. Then Dan turned to me and pointed to the TV screen. "What's the score?" he asked. *Does he think I'm drunk, or is he teasing me?* I told him the number. I wondered if I should start following sports just so I could have a better conversation with him. Then he said, "I'm going to grab a bite." He didn't ask me to come along. Instead of being friendly and asking to join him, I said, "Okay. I'll go home." I didn't know how to be social around a single man, and he wasn't any help. Looking back, we were both pretty bad at liking each other.

Even though I was not thinking about getting back into a romantic relationship, my friends hoped I'd click with someone. When Rachel and Michael wanted to introduce me to someone, I always said yes. One night, Rachel had arranged a casual dinner at her house with Noel; he was a couple of years younger than I was, and I'd seen him at work. She was not pushy about it, but she thought there'd be no harm in everyone having dinner together and seeing what happened. Then nothing happened.

A couple of years later, Rachel again set me up on a date, this time with her CEO. This was much clearer to me as a date: my first blind date. We met during lunch at Starbucks at the Galleria Mall in East Cambridge. Unsure of what to talk about, we focused on our work—easy for me, but our conversation didn't flow. There were many uncomfortable silences. Other than work, we had nothing to talk about. For sure, we didn't hit it off. I also wasn't attracted to him and didn't see us being a couple. I wondered why Rachel thought we might be compatible. Probably just because he was single, eligible, and employed.

When I was thirty-one, Michael, along with his wife, introduced me to his college buddy, Phil, who lived in Maine. The four of us spent a weekend together. At one point, Phil said to me, "Do you want to take a boat ride?" I loved boat rides, so I nodded. He smiled.

"Why don't you two just go? We're going to get ice cream," Michael said. Phil showed me the way down to the river. The sun shone in a cloudless blue sky—perfect. Except romance did not linger in the air at all. Phil talked about his political ambition, which was my least favorite topic. He didn't have anything else to say, and I didn't either. For most of the boat ride, we sat in silence.

Three years after the one-night debacle with Dan, another

guy at the office approached me. "Hey, I have tickets to see Paul Simon. Want to come?" I liked Alex—we hung out in the same social group, and he was always friendly to everyone.

"That would be cool," I said, not giving it a second thought. I felt comfortable with him and didn't think to ask about paying for the ticket.

We grabbed pizza beforehand—Alex's suggestion. During dinner, he did most of the talking. I felt safe with him and was happy just to listen. At the concert, I enjoyed all the songs, though I didn't know most of them and felt a bit awkward. I tried not to let that bother me. Alex, on the other hand, knew all the tunes, quietly singing along in a sweet voice. We didn't speak to each other the whole time. After the concert, he walked me to my door. I said goodbye and left him. It didn't occur to me that this might have been a date. I assumed we were just friends.

A few weekends later, Alex needed to drop off his sister's car in Connecticut, and he asked me to come along. I said yes and thought that it might be fun to go on a road trip with a friend. During the weekend, I met his parents, who lived nearby. He took me to the beach, and we took the Amtrak back to Boston. We listened to music together on our iPods all the way back.

"What's a song you like?" Alex asked.

Ugh. I couldn't name a single song. This was one of those times I wished I'd been born in the United States and that English was my first language. Then I might be better at knowing song names, having grown up with them. We went back to sitting silently together on the train, not making any special connection.

A few weeks later, Alex approached my desk. "My sister

and I are going camping this weekend. Want to come?" He smiled at me.

"Sounds fun!" I thought it would be cool to hang out with him and his sister.

"Can we use your car to go?" he asked.

I didn't grow up driving. My family couldn't afford to get a second car when I was in high school. Only years later, when I had a job and made enough money, did I finally buy my first automobile. I rarely used it, though, because I could walk most places that I needed or wanted to go, and I also preferred public transportation so that I wouldn't have to worry about parking, which is not great in Boston.

"Sure. Of course."

Kim and Barbara, two girlfriends at work, heard that we were going camping for the weekend.

"You're going on a camping trip with Alex?" Kim asked when the three of us were sitting in a meeting room getting ready for a working session together.

"Yeah."

"Just you guys?"

"And his sister."

The two women, both friends with Alex and me, looked at me with wide-open eyes. I didn't really think about what it might mean.

When we started out, I drove first and almost got into an accident. At one point, I was changing lanes to the right. I didn't see a car in my blind spot. As I shifted to the right, a loud honk sounded.

"Watch out," Alex said. I swirled back to my lane. My heart raced. I'd almost gotten us killed.

"You okay?" both Alex and his sister asked.

"I think so."

"Want me to drive?" Alex leaned forward.

I happily gave up the driver's seat. Alex took over, and the three of us remained silent.

Once we got set up at a campsite, Alex made a fire so that we could cook hamburgers, and we all sat around it. Alex turned to me. "You said you like *Gilmore Girls*, right?"

"Yes, I do."

"Great show. Do you remember the time when they talked about—?" First, I didn't hear what he said clearly. Second, where did he get the idea that I liked that show? I didn't remember telling him. Third, I had only watched two episodes, which for me was a lot for a TV show.

I felt bad and embarrassed. I didn't ask him to repeat himself. Instead, I just tried to change the subject. "Hmm. I don't remember that. I don't think I saw that." Alex went on to talk to his sister. I sat quietly again, watching the amazing color from the fire.

Later that night at the campsite, when we were getting ready to go to sleep, Alex knocked on my tent and asked me to follow him to an open, grassy area. He pointed to the sky. "Can you see the stars?"

I had just taken off my contact lenses and couldn't see anything, but I didn't tell him that. Then he took my hand and drew the constellation Cassiopeia on the back of it. I'd seen the movie *Serendipity*, where John Cusack did the same thing on Kate Beckinsale's hand when he finally met her again after searching for her all over New York City, but I didn't know what to say. Distracted by not being able to see, I just wanted to crawl into my sleeping bag and didn't respond to Alex sharing an intimate moment with me. After a few minutes of silence, we returned to our separate tents.

During that weekend, Alex, his sister Amy, and I went to the highest point of the mountain in the park to see the sunrise. He gave me a hug as the sun came up. Then we sat next to each other watching the sun become whole. The sunset was amazing. The array of reds and orange blending together looked spectacular. The round shape of the sun slowly came into view, spreading light to the rest of the world. I didn't think of Alex at all.

That evening, Alex planned a sunset kayak trip. The three of us got to the dock, and the guide instructed us to wear life-jackets—a great idea because I didn't know how to swim, and we were about to venture into the Atlantic Ocean, but I didn't hesitate. Alex and I shared a kayak, with me in front. Off we went into the ocean and the sunset. I felt so at peace. Alex told me later he'd gone kayaking with an ex-girlfriend once, and they'd gotten into a fight, which had ruined the experience. He liked how I always smiled and seemed to enjoy life. It seemed like it had been just a few minutes when the guide told everyone to turn around and head back to the dock.

"We don't want to be out here when it's completely dark."

We were going against the tide, so I had to paddle hard to make any progress. *Thank goodness Alex is with me.* I turned to look at him, and we smiled at each other.

I followed him around all weekend, letting him plan all the activities and cook all the meals, but I never considered how much effort he put into our trip. I also didn't think about why he was doing all this with me. I had never assumed, and he had never spelled it out for me. A few months later, I saw him with someone who ended up becoming the woman of his life. I was glad he'd found someone who truly loved him. We all stayed friends.

Right after hanging out with Alex, Derick came along, who made his intentions very clear.

"Hey, I have tickets to a play at the ART. Want to come?" Derick held up a pair of tickets.

"I love plays. I'd love to go," I said.

On the day of the play, we met at Casablanca, a couple of blocks away from the theater. The basement restaurant was known for its giant wall mural depicting the characters in *Casablanca* and was a stop for movie and theatergoers in Harvard Square.

"You look nice," he said when I walked in.

"Thanks." It was sweet of him to say that.

"Want to order some drinks?"

"I'll have a glass of red wine."

Derick paid for the drinks, and afterward we walked to the theater. I said nothing but enjoyed watching the play. After the show, I politely said goodnight and took the T home.

This went on a few more times, with Derick inviting me to shows and buying me drinks or sometimes dinner. We watched three or four shows together, and I always had a great time. But for some reason, I never thought of him as more than a friend. Clueless me.

On our last outing together, Derick suggested we grab drinks afterward at Casablanca before ending the night. We sat at the bar next to each other. I took a sip of my red wine. All of a sudden, Derick gave me a forceful kiss on my cheek. I was speechless. I got up and left. I didn't like this particular Derick.

When I think about all the men I'd been with after Chris, I had to wonder how much my quietness, timidity, and cluelessness were related to schizophrenia. Or perhaps the part of my personality and behavior that triggered schizophrenia in the first place still remained in me and prevented me from meeting people.

I also didn't know anything about dating. As an only child and a teenager, I grew up on my own without any role models to learn about relationships and love, while my parents focused on making a living. I didn't see much of them at home. I wasn't able to connect with single men more than what went on at work. My outgoing work personality contrasted greatly with my more private, personal one. My two major ex-boyfriends, Chris and Oliver, had been pretty upfront about liking me, and they had made the first moves. Earlier on in college, relationships were simple: You like me. I like you. Let's go out.

"No one ever specifically asked me out on a date," I'd say later to Rachel. In my thirties, because of all the problems I'd had, the timing for a relationship was not right for me, and I wasn't mentally ready to meet someone significant. My focus was primarily on work and friendships. I couldn't handle anything more than being with myself and being single.

Years later, I still kept in touch with a few of these men. Some of them became friends rather than just single guys. Dan and Alex both got married and had adorable kids. Other men moved away. I was happy for everyone who had found their center in life. I didn't regret meeting them. Unlike other single women friends of mine, I didn't feel I'd never meet anyone or wonder if I was unlikable. Quite the opposite, I felt fortunate to have had the chance to go out with a lot of different people.

I felt I was liked by men even though these meetings hadn't led to any relationships. They were the wrong people at the wrong time.

It would take some time for me to get to know myself better and to feel confident, comfortable, and honest about who I was. Without knowing myself and feeling good about what I was all about, I couldn't get to know another person and include him in my life in any way. That would come later.

— Part 2 —

FLOURISH

8

COMPUTER VERSUS HUMAN

In 2015, at age forty-one, thirteen years after breaking up with Chris, I went on OkCupid, the first dating website I ever used, because Rachel had used it and had found a husband there. I got more comfortable with the idea of online dating as a source for meeting men and became curious about other dating websites and apps—how they worked and what algorithms they used to determine how two people could be a good match. I wondered if being on multiple websites and apps would result in my meeting a lot more men.

OkCupid matched people using questions such as "Can you date someone messy?" "Do you like to wear a costume for Halloween?" "Would you rather cook your own food or order takeout?" "Are you spiritual or religious?" "What do you prefer to swim in?" "How are you feeling about the 2020 election?" The website used a variety of questions from serious to casual to silly. I answered some and skipped others. Certain questions were easier to answer than others. I also kept some of the answers private so that only I could see my answers relating to politics, religion, and sex, which I preferred to have a conversation about rather than summarily reveal on a profile.

I also had to answer what my ideal guy's answers would be to these questions. *What if he were clean or messy? And how important will my cleanliness be to him?* Would I want to be unmatched with someone who answered he was messy because he did not put his dirty socks in the hamper? I thought if a man was kind and messy, I would still like to meet him. But if a man expected me to pick up his dirty socks every day, I wasn't so sure. *Who talks about dirty socks on the first date anyway?* As a neat person, I felt I could date either a messy or a neat man. A man could say he only dates messy women. In that case, we wouldn't be matched. As I went on answering hundreds of questions for both of us, I gave "him" plenty of latitude.

OkCupid took these answers plus how you ranked the importance of the questions and calculated a matching percentage. Each man, or each profile, had a percentage of "matchness" to my profile. There were literally thousands of questions, and I only answered about a hundred or so. Initially, I liked the fun and simple questions but soon realized that hard questions were equally important. For fun, I liked the beach over the mountains. But more importantly, I wasn't religious and didn't want to date someone who would make that a requisite in a relationship. The more experienced I became, I used the numbers they came up with as just one of the many indicators of a man's compatibility with me. I believed there was something between two human beings that might not be quantified into a neat mathematical equation and presented by a simple number.

The second website I tried was eHarmony, which had a very lengthy setup process. I sat in front of my computer and took on a three-hour assessment before I could be matched to anyone. They wanted to know my personality and preferences. The assessment included picking out words I preferred as well as multiple-choice questions like on OkCupid. After a day or two, I received my first three matches. I decided to contact one of them. The way it worked was I could ask him questions, and when he answered them, he had the opportunity to ask me questions as well. After that, we were able to message each other freely. Unfortunately, I didn't like their heavy-handed approach to the initial interaction between two people, probably because I'd started on OkCupid first and resonated more with how they fostered the dating process. I soon stopped using eHarmony.

Two very popular dating apps were Tinder and Bumble, which had no websites at all. I had no trouble signing up with either of these because doing so was quick and easy. Similar to OkCupid and eHarmony, I had to upload my photos. But instead of writing a full profile, I only needed to add captions or a few short sentences about myself if I wanted to. The way these apps worked was founded on how we meet people in real life: based on first impressions of how someone looks. On my phone, I saw pictures of different men. If I liked a guy's photos or short blurbs, I could show I liked him by swiping right. When I didn't like someone, I passed that person by swiping left. Matches happened when both people liked each other and swiped right. Bumble worked similarly to Tinder, with one additional rule, which was that women had twenty-four hours to message first after being matched. If I didn't write within twenty-four hours, that match disappeared. After I wrote the first message, the man also had twenty-four hours to decide if he wanted to respond.

After about fifty swipe-lefts, I saw a man who went to UC

Berkeley and Columbia Business School. Cute. Nice pictures. Cool. So I swiped right. So did he, and we matched.

"*Nee how ma*," he texted first. That annoyed me.

"Hi. How are you?" I replied.

"How do you say 'fine' in Chinese?" I didn't like how he assumed I was Chinese. To me, it was like assuming every white man is from England. But, hey, I didn't want to read into it too much.

"*Han how*. Lucky that I know Chinese to answer your question. It's a beautiful day, isn't it? Just finished brunch with a girlfriend. Maybe heading to the Museum of Fine Arts." I tried to change the subject to see if I could find the goodness in him.

"Very nice outside. How do you say 'let's get naked' in Chinese?"

"Maybe it's a bit early to learn that." I was totally offended now. I wanted to end the conversation as soon as possible.

He responded with a crying face emoji.

"Yes, unfortunately! So you are interested in Chinese and getting naked." I texted my final thought and unmatched him.

Seriously, I had to laugh.

To make sure I didn't miss anything, I searched online for the top dating apps and tried almost every one on the list. Another dating site, Coffee Meets Bagel, curated matches daily, but I found the pace a bit slow. While Hinge found singles in my Facebook network, Happn showed singles near me in real time as I moved around town. I didn't get attached to any of these dating apps because I didn't see anyone interesting. There weren't that many men and no quality matches for me.

I knew that plenty of other online dating websites and apps existed, and after all the ones I sampled, I also had a pretty good idea about how they worked. Contrary to what I thought, however, I didn't meet more people. I just started seeing the same men on multiple dating sites. More was not better in terms of choice or quality.

I went back to mostly using OkCupid because I was used to how it worked. Against my general rules of not paying for anything on my iPhone, I paid for an additional premium A-list feature so I could see who liked me. Rachel and I discussed this option in detail.

As a very general rule, men like to make the first move. Because of that, and after scrolling through profile after profile, the men I chose by liking their profiles might not have even seen I had an interest in them because of the way the basic system was designed. I realized it was a waste of time to look at men's profiles and mark that I liked them first. With the paid feature, I could see who was interested in me, and I therefore only needed to look at profiles of men who already expressed a desire to connect with me. I felt this was more efficient. I didn't need to see a world of men. I just needed one good one.

Still, having the A list felt like a shortcut or cheating. Michael disagreed when I told him this. "Cheating or not, I call it curiosity. Why not? I'm sure you'll find the guy who enjoys watching clouds with you. If not, you'll still enjoy a beautiful day."

Rachel said, "That doesn't sound like cheating to me. Just data gathering."

After a few months of using these apps, I saw by chance on Facebook that an acquaintance was working at a matchmaking company. Curious about what this entailed, I connected with her and asked her what she did at work. She told me she arranged blind dates for singles. The idea of having someone arrange dates and do searches for me had great appeal—human brain versus computer algorithm. Who would win? It also might mean that I could meet a different pool of men from those I'd been meeting via dating apps.

I made an appointment to speak officially to someone at her company who handled new clients. The woman at FindLove answered all my questions. They'd assign a match-maker to me based on what I was looking for. The matchmaker would screen potential candidates who met my criteria and set up first dates, including a place to meet up. These would be blind dates. Unlike using dating websites, which were completely free, this service required a huge and serious investment, close to five hundred dollars per date. I thought if I was serious and wanted to meet someone of quality, I should give a matchmaker a try.

A few weeks later, I was assigned to Dorothy, my very own matchmaker. She set up a time to meet online through Zoom in order to get to know me better. Dorothy had big hazel eyes, wore her hair pulled up into a long brown ponytail, and told me she loved yoga. She lived in Nantucket and loved the island. She looked to be around my age, possibly a bit younger. I liked her energy immediately. She told me this process would get better as we continued to work with each other. It took time to get to know a person to nail down exactly what they were looking for and what was attractive for a match. Both my criteria and chemistry were at play. After a one-hour video call, she sent me a huge list of questions via email. She wanted to know everything about me and what my close friends thought of me. Rachel put together five reasons she thought someone should date me. Dorothy also asked about my availability for the next month or so. Then she was off to her searches.

After a couple of weeks, I hadn't heard back from her. I got impatient and contacted her for an update.

"The search takes time," she said. "I want to thoroughly research a good match for you. Don't worry. I'll contact you when I have someone." I told myself to be patient and stop thinking about it.

Seven weeks later, while I was in a work meeting one morning, I received a text from Dorothy: "Hello, Mindy. How are you? Are you still available this Thursday? I have an amazing guy for you! He's smart, witty, a foodie, and up for pretty much anything. Would love to send you both out Thursday at 7 p.m. to play some games and grab a beverage. Sound good?"

I responded, "Hey! Good to hear from you. Yes, I am still free Thursday night. That's awesome! Games? I hope it's not trivia. I am horrible at that!"

"Yeah! It's a game café in Brookline. So much fun! And there are many options for games. Grab a bunch and get to know Edward, your new friend. I'll set it up."

A few days later, my matchmaker told me I had a first date. I couldn't sit still. I asked Dorothy for more information about the man, but she would not give me any more details. She wanted me to get to know him the traditional way: by meeting and talking to each other in person. Without knowing anything about him except his name, I felt quite giddy. I could not contain my excitement.

Dorothy told me the location of our meeting, not a place I would ever have picked. In fact, even though the café was in my neighborhood, I'd never noticed it.

"Games," I said to my friends.

"My husband and I spent our whole first year of dating

playing Trivial Pursuit and not talking," Rachel said. "There's hope for meeting over games. There are many more games than trivia. And have a drink to get the tongue loosened!"

"Games can be fun," Michael agreed. "I went to a party last fall where they had games and found I can be quite competitive."

"It sounds like the place is close to home, so that's good. Plus you're there to get to know him—the game stuff is just a distraction," Rachel said. "I had a friend whose name is Edward. He's a good guy. Wonder if this is the same Edward. He could be the one I know ... LOL. Oh, wait: the Edward I know lives in Europe. Have fun!"

"Haha! Maybe he's here for a visit," I responded.

When I first got the text about this blind date, I Googled "Edward" since that was all I had. I was trying to learn who he might be. But other than his first name, I didn't have any details. I also told my friends the date was probably going to be embarrassing because I was not good with games. I never played games growing up, so I would be out of my element. But I would definitely have a couple of drinks!

Was I making a mistake? I hadn't screened him, so I would just have to trust Dorothy. I might be able to beat him in card games. I wondered if I could focus on the game and forget about the guy. The date began to be fun to think about, and my this-is-a-mistake gut feeling disappeared. It became a mystery to be solved.

At 5 p.m. on the day of the blind date, I got the following text from Dorothy: "Hey, Mindy! Get ready for your upcoming date with Edward at 7:30. What will you be wearing?"

"Hey! Just about wrapping up with work. Can finally

relax and get in the mood for the blind date. Wearing a blue and white striped summer dress with white Vans. Should I wear my favorite jewelry too?"

"Edward is wearing a blue polo-style shirt, jeans, and red shoes. Will have a red strap attached to his camera."

Red shoes? Okay. This was intriguing. Definitely unique. At first, I thought she was just being supportive when she asked what I was wearing. Now I understood this was her way of helping us recognize each other.

Thirty minutes later, I heard from Dorothy again. "Remember, Edward is a foodie. He loves to try new restaurants and check out different food. He's for sure adventurous. He's upbeat and loves to talk. He loves witty banter and conversations. He's from Canada, but his family is from Asia. He's very close with his family and loves being able to spend time with them."

Edward was there when I arrived at the game café. That impressed me: the quality of being on time. He had a big smile on his face when he saw me. I immediately noticed he was short and stocky, and I knew I was not attracted to him physically. He would be a friend.

He bought me a smoothie because this game café had no liquor license. He asked me what game I wanted to play. Being in the moment and taking chances, I picked Risk. We sat down near the front next to the window, away from other people. He explained the rules. We set it up and continued talking for the rest of the hour.

"I work a lot. I think too much. I am a bit burned out. When I'm not working, I like to play video games," Edward said after telling me about working as a strategy consultant at a well-known global firm.

Smart. Hardworking. Hm, video games? "Oh, maybe you should cut back on your working hours?" I suggested.

"Yeah, I should. I am trying to live better."

As we walked out of the game café at the end of the date, after a few awkward silent seconds, Edward smiled and turned to me. "How about we hug? I am a hug kind of guy!" I was relieved to hear that and thought, *He knew what to do.* We hugged and said our goodbyes. I immediately realized that the benefit of having Dorothy was also that she would manage what happens after a date. I didn't have to decide right away and give out my number at the end of the first date.

I summarized Edward to my friends: smart and articulate, talkative, studies health sciences, works in software consulting but wants to start something new and stop doing strategy consulting. Says the food in Boston sucks and Toronto has better food. Believes having a Zipcar membership is not the same as having one's own car. Thinks Trump might get reelected because he's still speaking to his base. Needs only three to five hours of sleep. Goes to bed at 1 a.m. Thinks the game café is a weird place to meet. Gave me a hug when we said our goodbyes.

We'd had a high-quality conversation; he had a great personality, and I admired his passion for his work. But I wasn't attracted to him physically and felt no chemistry.

Dorothy had found the core of what I was looking for and was not off by much. But no one can predict chemistry. I'd had a great time with him and was happy it was such a good experience. I looked at the FindLove survey on my phone. I needed to reply. *Do I want to see him again and give him my number?* I didn't want to waste our time if I was not interested, so I declined to see him again and gave my reasons.

When I met with Rachel and Michael to talk about my date, she said, "I know how a guy looks is important, but looks change. A little change in lifestyle and time at the gym can totally change the way one looks. When I first met my husband, he was a stick, but after going to the gym, he's more buff. A little love handle! All I'm saying is keep an open mind. Sounds like you had fun regardless. I liked him up until the part where he said Boston food sucks. Then he lost all of my support. Glad you had fun, though. And, wow, Dorothy seems like she knows what she's doing."

Michael said, "Attraction can grow."

Rachel nodded. "But if you're not attracted to him, then you're not."

I felt bad. I had trouble being honest about my very opinionated feelings based on just one date, even though Rachel sided with me. I was glad she agreed.

"Yes, I'm moving on."

A few weeks later, Dorothy messaged me again. She had another date for me. Again, she didn't tell me anything about him. I worked until an hour before the date. Then I got myself ready. This time, she didn't tell me what he was wearing ahead of time but made a reservation under her name. An hour before my date, I got the following text from her:

"Frank is a doctor and consultant. He has a passion for cooking and trying new foods. He loves to play around in the kitchen. He is well-mannered and polished but not someone stuffy. He has two children and is very close with them. He enjoys cooking with his sons. They recently went to a cooking class together. He's looking for someone open-minded and adventurous."

I showed up at the place where I was told and asked for a

reservation under "Dorothy." "I'm here for a blind date," I told the young host.

"Oh, how exciting. I'll put you in a corner to have some privacy."

I followed her and sat at a table for two away from the crowd.

"Here you go." The young woman brought a man to my table a few minutes later, gave me a wink, and quietly walked away.

"Hi. Are you here for Dorothy?" the man asked.

"Yes, hi, I'm Mindy." The first impression was that he was pleasant and cute. *I've seen him on OkCupid. Small dating world.*

"Oh, good. I'm Frank. Nice to meet you." He sat down next to me, not too far and not too close. We both ordered drinks, gin and tonic for me and whisky for him. We made some small talk about how quaint the restaurant was.

"So what do you do? What did you study? Where was school for you?" I liked when a man asked questions. It showed that he was interested. Those were also questions I would ask him.

"I went to school in Ithaca. Have you been? Beautiful place. I studied electrical engineering at Cornell, but I don't tell people that anymore."

"Why?"

"Because I haven't done a single day of work in that field."

He laughed. "How come?"

"The hot jobs for EEs who concentrated in signal processing were with cell phone companies like Motorola. I interviewed with them. I saw the cubicles and thought to myself, *This is not for me.* I studied EE because that's what my dad did." I didn't want Frank to get the impression that I didn't appreciate Cornell. "But I had an excellent education. I did a lot of math and learned to have a logical mind. Cornell was a lot more than just EE to me."

I took a sip of my drink and relaxed a bit. "Now I work for a small software consulting company—specifically for healthcare." I felt that was a mouthful. "I was a project manager, and now I'm in business development."

"Do you like it?"

"I do. I love the people I work with." Work, to me, was always about the people. "I also love the work itself. Work has always been one of the centers of my life. It doesn't take over my life, but it's an important part of me. And I'm lucky. I've never felt like I was working for the money. Money just came with the work I did."

When I asked Frank the same question, he didn't quite have an easy answer. He was experimenting with being a masseuse. "I like feeling someone's body reacting to my touch." He also spent his free time at a dance studio. "I like hanging out with dancers even though I don't dance." Then he told me that he lied about not having been married when he was already married to this woman. Then he had to go through a fake wedding for his in-laws when they visited later. That was when I decided that he was not the one for me.

9

BUILDING CONFIDENCE

I learned pretty quickly that dating was all about learning about my date and telling him about me. After a few dates, I quickly found out what I liked to talk about when I spoke about myself as topics like work came up. Work was an important part of my identity.

The first company I worked for when I got out of school was called Sapient, with about four hundred employees at the time. Something about it made it feel like an extension of college, probably because I was mostly surrounded by people my age recruited from top schools all over the country. There were enough experienced managers leading young people like me straight out of college.

I had realized pretty quickly that once I entered the working world, I had to buy new clothes. The dress code—business suits—was written in the employment agreement that I signed. I had one black jacket from college and wore that to all of my job interviews. So one weekend before I started working, I headed to the Wrentham Outlets south of Boston and was immediately overwhelmed by all the brand-name stores. In DKNY, a dark-brown jacket and skirt suit caught my eye. Simple and modern. Then I looked at the price tag. Wow! It cost two hundred and fifty dollars. I'd never bought anything that expensive for myself. I figured I had to spend money to make money. Wanting to look the part at work, I swallowed hard and handed my credit card to the cheerful young cashier. By the end of the day, I came close to maxing out my credit. I spent several thousand dollars on five new suits and blouses, one for each day of the week. I planned to wear them week after week and hoped no one cared since I had just spent the most money I'd ever had in one day on clothing. I hoped that the DKNY and Jones New York suits might visually compensate for my inexperience and freshness in the corporate world.

For my first job, I didn't get a desk. My first few projects were Sapient's Rapid Implementation Plans (RIPs), full-week workshops with clients in a large open room with wall-to-wall whiteboards.

A RIP leader addressed a small group of us. "Tomorrow, we start at seven. Clients will be here around eight for breakfast. The first working session should kick off at eight thirty. Here are the topics. We should end at six. All right, let's prep."

Not being a morning person, I was thankful for my alarm clock. My job was to write down what everyone was saying, all twenty of them. I sat in the back of a large square room in front of a computer set up specifically for capturing notes. *Thank goodness I type fast.* As I typed out what was discussed, I had to simultaneously format the ideas. I learned all the short keys for PowerPoint and Excel. The notes were presented right after each working session. Sometimes, the conversations were captured in real time on the whiteboard. Good thing my handwriting was neat. I picked up tricks like alternating the marker color every line so it was easier to read what I wrote on the whiteboard from a distance. When I didn't know how to spell a word, I fudged it, which was the only time my handwriting was illegible. I learned to be quick on my feet, literally and figuratively, and very attentive to what was happening in the room at all times.

The RIP days were long. By the time I went home, it was dark outside, and I was exhausted, but I learned about new business ideas like how ordinary people can buy gas due to the deregulation of retail gas or how they can buy stock on their own on the internet for the first time in the United States. Every night, I slept like a baby.

I was assigned a longer-term project when I got a desk. After these short RIPs, I became part of a pack of about forty people who worked on what they called Project Rio. I sat in an open space where I could see what everyone was doing. Most of the time, everyone was in front of a computer screen typing away. Sapient didn't have cubicles. Since this was my first job, I didn't think about privacy. This was the norm for me, and I liked it.

Our team meeting started at nine in the morning. I usually arrived at work five minutes early. We stood in a circle around a plan on the whiteboard and spoke one by one about what we did and what we were going to do. When it was my turn, I felt nervous. I wondered if everyone in the room could hear my quickening, loud heartbeats. *Speak louder and be clear,* I told myself. I hadn't done too much public speaking, but with time, I finally got the hang of it.

Starting as a software developer, I understood some of

the principles of computer science from school. But I really learned what I needed to do on the job. I was coding in VB and C++. I was not particularly excellent at coding, but I was very good at getting help and asking questions.

One day, when I'd been on the Rio project for a month or so, I called over one of the managers. "Hey, Bernard, can I ask you a question?" He was a couple of years older and a software architect on the project. He walked over to my desk and then looked at my screen.

"This is what I did, but I'm getting a compiling error," I explained.

Bernard grabbed the mouse, scrolling through my code. "Can you run the software program? Show me what you did to get the error." I repeated what I did in front of him.

"I think this is your problem." Bernard pointed to a typo I had in a function. Because of that, my program used a different function.

"Ah. Let me try again ... Oh, it works. Thank you."

"No problem." Bernard walked back to his desk, not too far from mine. Even though it was my title, coding was only one part of my job. I learned how to collaborate with people and solve problems.

"I'm hungry," one of my colleagues said while loosening his tie at around 6 p.m.

"Let's order some dinner." Our manager did a quick head-count and called a restaurant.

A few minutes later, huge plates of sushi were delivered to our team area. Everyone took a break and enjoyed the raw fish and vinegar rice. Then we all got back to our computers and continued to type for the rest of the evening. People who were married with kids looked at us college graduates with amazement, probably thinking, *Don't expect me to eat dinner and sleep here.* But we all loved our work. "Working hard and playing hard" was definitely our motto.

When deadlines weren't hanging over us, some of us spent our free time together.

"Movie, guys?" Michael, a database administrator on the project, asked.

"What's playing? What about dinner first?" said Rachel, a project manager.

Michael called out, "*The Avengers.*"

We were all about work, food, and then fun.

"Chinatown? The pho place? Tasty, cheap, and fast," I added.

After dinner and a movie, we were right back together at work the next day. The people I met back in 1997—Rachel, Michael, and a handful of others—became lifelong friends. Besides making personal friends, I started building a professional network of contacts.

One Monday morning, a client manager I worked with came over to my desk. "The chief technology officer wants to speak to you."

I was surprised as I'd never spoken directly to him the entire time I worked on our project. My mind went blank, steeling myself for any criticism he might have. I knocked on his door.

"Come in, Mindy." Mr. Smith, an older gentleman, had been with the organization for many years and was very well respected. "I'm glad you came. I want to thank you in person."

I was relieved. I didn't say anything but politely smiled.

"The project you're working on is critical to our organization, and I know about the disagreements among the team.

Some people didn't believe in the project, but I've heard very positive feedback from the manager this week. He and you are working together very well now. You've won him over." I nodded. "Things are going well. Thank you." I wished I had better words, but I didn't.

"Thank *you*," he responded. "Keep up the great work." Seeing it was the end of our conversation, I got up and left the room.

Slowly, one day at a time through work, I built self-confidence and self-worth, something I lacked because I was so young and new to the working world.

I didn't go to prom in high school, so I'd never gone shopping for that fancy dress. Parties were not something that I grew up knowing about as a child of Taiwanese immigrants. I focused on school work and part-time jobs as a teenager and college student. However, during the Christmas holiday, Sapient threw a party for everyone at the Children's Museum, so this was my chance to experience my first formal party. I wore a strappy brown velvet gown with matching stilettos that I found a week before. I put on pearl earrings, a bracelet, and a necklace. Everyone looked amazing. Women in long dresses— mostly in black but a few in bright colors. Men in suits and ties. I walked around and chatted with everyone I knew, which, to my amazement, added up to twenty or so people. Artwork on display added to the festive air as I walked around snacking on fabulous hors d'oeuvres like deviled eggs, rustic Tuscan bruschetta, and bacon-encased mushrooms. Another year, the holiday party was held at the State House of Massachusetts. A live band played seasonal songs on marble floors under the sky-lit golden dome of the massive rotunda. Historical paintings and sculptures from colonial times lined the halls.

Another year, we did so well that Sapient took everyone to Disney in Orlando. Rachel and I shared a room. We saw the amazing nighttime, brightly lit parades, went on rides, and watched our colleagues perform an Irish dance onstage. We had a blast.

It was a great time to work at a consulting company during the dot-com bubble. Businesses thrived, and everyone made a lot of money. Sapient even gave its employees stock options. At one point, my net worth could buy a nice apartment in Back Bay. But in my twenties, I was too young to know that I should diversify by selling some stocks and buying real estate. In 2002, a mere five years into my job, the bubble burst, and all that employee stock went down to almost nothing. I was not surprised when I was laid off. It was a business, after all.

When I first decided to work for Sapient, I didn't realize the impact it would have on me: lifelong friends, a professional network, the ability to think on my feet and work in an open culture, learning and making use of technology. By luck, I couldn't have asked for a better first job to become a young professional and, therefore, a confident and well-rounded young adult.

I also learned about personal finance at Sapient, one of the best personal gains from a job. Having a steady income meant I could pay off my college debts and contribute to a 401(k) with the company matching donations, even though I didn't make any money from selling my company stocks. Everyone around me seemed to be thinking about investing. So I did that and bought a few stocks too. Without knowing the benefit of compound interest, I took full advantage of what I was learning and saved and invested young and early. This habit benefited me later in life.

Growing up without extra money was a blessing in disguise. Careful with spending as a teenager in New Jersey, I knew my family was tight with money, while Dad worked double shifts as a mechanical engineer at a food processing company. I knew I was different from most of the teenagers at my high school. We didn't have a big house; we lived on the border of Millburn township. I didn't get a car when I got my license like most seniors at Millburn High School. Instead, I continued to walk to school and depend on my best friend, Rose, to take me places.

I learned about work ethics from my father. I spent my free time babysitting. When summer came, I worked as an office assistant for my fencing coach's printing company. At Cornell, I worked as a computer consultant at various computer labs on campus. I picked up as many shifts as I could during my free time. I hadn't asked my dad for money since I'd been a teenager. Even during college, knowing he was already paying for my expensive Ivy League tuition, we both took out additional loans to cover the difference that he couldn't pay each semester. I wanted to lighten his load as much as I could even if it was just a tiny drop in a bucket.

After Sapient, I felt that I had broad exposure to different industries—energy, finance, and healthcare—but didn't have enough depth of experience. I decided to work for a product company instead of continuing with consulting.

After a summer of free time—thanks to my savings—I found my second job with the help of my friend Jennifer. She worked at a small retail product company called ProfitLogic in Kendall Square. She forwarded my résumé to her hiring manager and kept checking in with her until they needed new hires.

During one interview, I was asked if I knew how to do a select statement to query data from a database. I didn't but answered, "I don't remember it by heart, but I can look it up if you give me the Oracle database book," which was true. A few days later, I got a job offer as a product configuration engineer.

ProfitLogic, a small company, had work cubicles for its employees. Assigned to one, I immediately felt the difference in corporate culture compared to Sapient. Here, a hundred or so people worked on one problem: calculating the optimal markdown price for a piece of clothing. To calculate that number, we used an engine, taking into consideration historical sales, forecasted sales, and scheduled promotions that would create a lift factor. At Sapient, I was used to building new software systems from scratch. But here, we had scientists, architects, developers, configuration engineers, and product managers all trying to perfect one specific business problem. Initially, I couldn't comprehend the need for all these people but then learned that this was what was needed to provide a product with in-depth business intelligence. For large retailers, the difference of a few dollars in markdown could lead to deltas in the millions.

After only a few weeks on the job, I approached my team leader. "I want to show you something," I said. I finally got my head wrapped around how all the different pieces worked in our product, while everyone else focused on their own specific areas. I created a comprehensive map that captured the information in the software. "I made a map of the data flow from the database, to the backend, to the middleware, to what's displayed on the screen." What I had learned from my first job helped, and I understood what I needed to do. He took a look and grabbed a product architect to view my spreadsheet.

"This is great. Just keep doing what you're doing," the architect said.

"It's missing these five pieces of data," I said to him. Being able to see how it all came together, I could identify the missing information and configure the product for a specific client. I felt useful seeing something that others hadn't.

"We can add those." Hearing what I needed, the product architect created a standard and easy way for other configuration engineers and me to do custom calculations based on what the client required. I was productive and worked on installing the markdown product for client after client.

Four years into my second job, ProfitLogic was acquired by Oracle Retail. I became one of the thousands who worked for this much larger operation and decided to look for another job. Reflecting on what I had done, retail held little interest for me. I always knew that I didn't have the heart to work on anything that moves and has blood, so anything in the health or medical field was out of the question, and I could certainly never be a doctor of any kind. But I liked the idea of helping people and being in a profession that could make a positive difference in people's lives. So second best would be to work on technology for healthcare companies. Perhaps I could help people that way. I turned to my friend Michael, who'd founded Medullan, a small consulting firm focused specifically on healthcare and technology. That sounded like the perfect match for what I wanted to do next.

I found myself working for smaller and smaller companies with each job. Medullan was the smallest company I had ever worked for. In Central Square, there were ten people in the office, including me, when I joined. I started as a project manager, finally putting my technical skills on the back burner.

When a client wanted to create the first healthcare cost-and-quality website in Massachusetts, I got very excited about creating something that would be the first of its kind. Imagine knowing how much something costs beforehand instead of getting a bill afterward.

"The client database administrator hasn't given us the test data we need. This is a major blocker," my architect told me one day, escalating this issue.

"Let me take a look at this and see if I can do something about it." I reprioritized my task list for the week and looked into this test data issue first.

A few days later, I met with the client lead and her database administrator and got all the details I needed. I spent the next week or so creating mock cost-and-quality data based on the relationship we had mapped out in an earlier model. I resolved the issue; having a technical background was particularly helpful when working with a team of technologists.

After one year on the job, Michael came to me with an amazing proposition. "How would you like to go to Trinidad for three months?" Medullan had an office there where we hired and trained software developers.

"Sure. Why not?" What a great opportunity to see a different part of the world and get away from Boston's cold winter. In November 2008, I happily packed t-shirts, shorts, sundresses, and flipflops and hopped on a plane.

Wesley, a developer at Medullan, volunteered to pick me up at the airport. He spotted me first as I walked out of the customs area. Cheri and Kavita, the managers at the office, made sure I got settled in at a house they'd rented for me conveniently located near the office. I quickly learned it was uncommon to walk anywhere. Hemraj, another developer, picked me up every morning to go to work, and Sean, another developer, dropped me off at home. With that kind of attention, I felt right at home.

I remembered being eager to learn when I first started out at Sapient. Now the tables were turned: everyone in the Trinidad office was much younger than me, and they were ready to soak up all the knowledge I had.

Outside of the office, I became the learner, eager to find out everything I could about this small Caribbean nation. One of my colleagues there gave me a blue steelpan, a musical instrument originating from Trinidad and Tobago. I loved having doubles for breakfast—street-food flatbread sandwiches with curried chickpeas—and KFC or curry chicken for dinner.

On weekends, I walked everywhere, even though I was told doing so was unsafe. When Michael came into town, the two of us took the maxi—a private minibus—to a mall or movie theater. Michael was even more adventurous than me, having traveled to many places in the world. It took us two hours to slowly travel to the movie theater while we chatted all the way, not noticing how long it was taking. On the way back, we stopped randomly at a small hole-in-the-wall restaurant for curry chicken, which we both enjoyed.

Kavita and Cheri found out that I loved beaches after I was there for a few weeks. "Do you want to go to Tobago? The beaches there are beautiful. The plane ticket is fifty dollars. We'll get a group together to go." Tobago is the sister island of Trinidad.

"Sounds great. Let's go."

On a Saturday morning, ten of us met at Trinidad's small airport. After a very short flight, we landed at an even smaller airport in Tobago. We checked into a nice hotel and headed to the nearby beach right away, where Ibrar, another technologist at Medullan, learned how to swim in the ocean and almost lost his wedding ring.

A woman on the beach offered to braid hair. I turned to Kavita, who had been with the company for almost as long as I was, about a year, and worked with me on the same projects. "Should I try it?"

She nodded. "If you do it, I'll do it with you." I wanted to try something new. I sat on a small wooden stool as this beautiful woman braided my straight, long black hair into tight cornrows. After she finished several hours later, I looked in the mirror and thought I looked awful! My face looked so big now that my hair was tightly nestled around my skull. And the braids hurt. After waiting around thirty minutes, I turned to Kavita. "You think it would be wrong for me to take the braids out? They really hurt." We looked at each other and laughed out loud.

After being in Trinidad for six weeks, I woke up one Saturday morning with rashes all over my body and a fever. I stayed in bed. I was not particularly good at getting help from doctors and didn't want to bother anyone. I don't remember how long I'd slept, feeling uncomfortable and hot when someone knocked on my door. Kavita stepped in and took a long look at me.

"Oh my God! You're sick. I'm going to take you to the doctor." She drove me to a yellow building. We took the stairs to an office on the second floor. Someone took my blood.

It turned out I had dengue, which people can die from. The doctor took my temperature and examined me. "It seems that it's almost passed." He prescribed some medicine for me anyway. Kavita then took me to a pharmacy. Someone behind a metal window filled my prescriptions. I took them home but didn't take any pills. I disliked taking medication and avoided taking it if I could help it, especially because I was in a foreign country. Who knew what was in these pills? Luckily, I simply slept off the illness.

Kavita, Cheri, Sean, Kalisha, and others also took me clubbing, or *liming*, as the Trinis would say. I listened to calypso and soca—calypso music that has a touch of soul in it. I watched in awe as people were dancing, or *wining*, as they call it.

My three-month stay in Trinidad went by quickly. Before I left, Kalisha invited me to her home and treated me to a dish called cascadura or cascadoux, made from a kind of catfish that is local to the island. According to the Trinidad legend, anyone who eats this fish will end their days on the island. "So you will have to come back to us," she said.

10

A SMALL BLADDER BUT A LARGE STOMACH

Over the years, I worked mainly at three companies, from Sapient to ProfitLogic (which later became part of Oracle Retail) to Medullan. My career has always been a source of fulfillment and stability. I learned that while work can change over time, the close friends I meet there will remain part of my life. Those friends have stood by me through my life as a single woman, and for that I am grateful.

At ProfitLogic, I eventually became part of a group of ten or so singles who frequented the bars in Faneuil Hall and Back Bay after work.

I learned that my bladder was useless when I started drinking. One night at Faneuil Hall, Michael started buying Bud Light for everyone. I must have downed two or three bottles in a short time. I went to the bathroom nonstop.

"Are you alright?" Michael asked, noticing how I kept leaving the table.

"Yes. Beer goes right through me apparently." I laughed.

"You guys go sing. I'll be right back." As the group went onstage to sing karaoke, I went to the bathroom again.

When I came back, I noticed that the guys from the office were talking to some girls I didn't know at the bar. *Guys will be guys.* I was happy that some action was happening and decided that the night was a success. *I'm going to enjoy the live music.*

One day, Rachel and I were hanging out with a couple of other friends from work. "We should start a steak club," Rachel said. Our first choice was Morton's The Steakhouse.

"Wait. Is the entrée just the steak?" I asked. Having never been to a fancy steak place, I was surprised that forty dollars just bought a piece of meat.

"Yes. You have to order sides separately," Michael said.

"I guess that's why it's a steakhouse."

A waiter came by with a large plate showing different cuts of meat. The portions were mostly large. I went for the smallest. Eating steak became a monthly adventure. After a year or so, we had dined at most of the steak restaurants in Boston.

"Let's plan for a holiday version." Instead of fancy company parties, we organized our own lavish party. Rachel reserved a large private room for us. About twenty of us showed up, and everyone looked great. It was extravagant. At least thirty empty wine bottles lined one side of the room. I had pulled out the dress I wore to the state house, and Rachel lent me her sparkling earrings. Everyone had steak. Rachel had center-cut sirloin. I had the smallest five-ounce ribeye. Alex had a bone-in that was as big as his head. Such excessive and merry eating and drinking. Glasses were refilled constantly. Somebody ordered desserts for everyone.

When our reservation for the private room ended, we decided to move to a club nearby. I completely engrossed myself in the music and danced nonstop with Rachel. I didn't know the songs, but that didn't stop me from having a blast. At the end of the night, Rachel and I shared a cab home. My head was spinning. My heart was racing. If Boston didn't shut down at 1 a.m., we would have danced longer.

Besides going out in large groups, hanging out one on one was the best way for me to get to know someone. Jasmine and I first met each other at Oracle Retail as project managers. She was single and a few years younger than me. We sat back to back in the office and hit it off right away. We ate alphabetically through Boston.

One day, after we'd known each other for a few months, Jasmine tapped my shoulder. "Doing anything after work?"

I shrugged. "What're you thinking? Walk around and get dinner together? What letter is it now? H?" Neither of us had a car, and I knew she loved walking around in Boston.

"Sounds great." She was up for doing anything. I saw myself in her.

A little after 5 p.m., Jasmine and I walked out of Davenport, our office in East Cambridge.

"Okay if we go to Helmand?" I asked. Located nearby in East Cambridge, Helmand was an Afghani restaurant named after Afghanistan's longest river.

She nodded. "I love that place. Best lamb chops ever."

We walked leisurely and chatted about the day. Then the topic switched to personal projects. At the time, we both owned small condos in Back Bay. Jasmine loved decorating her home. With her talent, she could be an interior designer or home organizer if she ever tired of working for software companies.

But then I noticed her slowing down. "Mindy, I feel lonely lately," she said in a quiet voice. Jasmine was generally optimistic and cheerful about her life, but I knew that everyone had moments like this. I hugged her.

"I thought you were happy being on your own. What happened?"

"Yeah, but my ex-boyfriend texted me, and I realized I still miss him."

"What did he say? Is he still single too?" Chris and I had a lingering phase as well. I understood what that felt like. But, like me, Jasmine was private about her relationships. We didn't dwell on our ex-boyfriends.

"He just said hi. I didn't ask him." She knew, like I did, that moving on was the best thing unless this guy was thinking about something more. It didn't sound like it, but I didn't judge. The people who know best how to handle their relationship are the two people involved. No one else.

"You want to start dating?" I asked.

"I don't really like online dating. There are so many weird guys out there. I want to focus my life on positive energy and remove all negative noises."

I nodded in agreement.

At Helmand, we joined the long line, typical of a work night. We didn't mind waiting and continued talking. Then we were seated near the window. We both ordered *chowpan*, the lamb chops. I asked Jasmine if she had any travel plans. We'd been to New York City, Nantucket, Martha's Vineyard, and even the Caribbean together.

"Our Aruba trip was awesome. Remember that? Four perfect days. Remember that clam and pasta dish we had across the street from the hotel?" Jasmine switched to a happier topic and brought us down memory lane.

"We totally lucked out. We didn't even plan that. So good. Again, we both ordered the same thing." I laughed. Then I added, "It's great that we can both sit around and do nothing. Just enjoying quality time with ourselves."

"Love that," Jasmine echoed.

After a very satisfying dinner, we headed to the Lechmere T stop and caught the train home. We lived three blocks from each other. Not only were we friends and coworkers, but we were also neighbors. On weekends, we sometimes called each other spontaneously and went for walks along the Charles River. That night, we hugged each other and said our goodbyes, knowing we'd see each other again in the morning.

Besides having friends who loved clubbing and those I hung out with one on one, I also had friends who were more family-oriented. Instead of bars and clubs, we met at backyards and parks.

Once a year, I went glamping with five of my girlfriends and their husbands and kids. Finding a weekend we were all free posed a challenge with kids' soccer games, playdates, and weekend classes. But we always made it happen for all nineteen of us, and there always seemed to be one more little one on the way.

As the only single person in the group, I was never made to feel like I stood out or was an oddball. I credited this to my amazing girlfriends whom I'd met at Sapient. Even though they were all married, we met regularly during the year for dinner. They'd take turns organizing our get-together. I was just one of the girls. I also enjoyed hearing about their lives with kids and husbands. They were just as eager to hear about my single life.

"We're living vicariously through you." They laughed. Part of what also made these relationships work was their open-minded, understanding husbands. They knew their wives needed girl time. A couple of times a year, I got to see the husbands too—all respectful and kind. One of them, Nick, was good friends with my ex-boyfriend, Chris. He'd helped me look for a new job. Another named Scott introduced me to his best friend from college, hoping that two people he liked would hit it off. I was among close married friends who didn't let my singleness get in the way of friendship. My girlfriends made me a priority in their lives.

As husbands and wives finished each other's jokes, I joined in on the fun. I was accepted by Rachel, Michael, Samantha, Zoe, Vara, Paige, and my other friends. And the kids, ranging from a baby to teenagers, all modeled after their parents, called me Auntie Mindy and hung out with me like I was part of their families.

"Zoe, can I catch a ride with you on Friday?" I asked one time when we were going camping. At the time, I had moved to Brookline, and Zoe lived around the corner. Two other families in the group also lived in Brookline.

"Of course. We're leaving around three. Can you come by then?" There would be five of us in the car plus everything we needed for the weekend.

Zoe and her husband always made me feel like part of the family. When I had to rehome my two cats because of my travel for work, and the fact that they often kept me up at night getting aggressive with each other with full-on hissing, I called Zoe to give me a ride to a shelter. Several days later, Zoe told me she saw me shaking when I gave my two cats back to the shelter. She didn't want to go inside with me because she was afraid she might cry.

Another time, I had to get a colonoscopy and needed someone to take me home from the hospital. I asked Zoe's husband, Nick, to pick me up, and he was there for me, no questions asked. When I later experienced symptoms of schizophrenia, I asked Zoe if I could spend the night at her home. That's how close I felt to her and her family. I was blessed to have friends like that so close by.

"Sounds good," I told her. At 3 p.m. on Friday, I brought my camping bag with me and walked to Zoe's house. She, her husband, and her kids were in the process of loading their car with bags of food, pillows, blankets, and clothes.

An hour later, we arrived at the campsite. Nick stopped the car in front of my cabin. "Are you going to be okay staying by yourself?" Zoe asked.

"I'll be fine. See you in a few minutes." I got the smallest cabin but was still pretty close to everybody. I dropped my bag inside, cleaned up a bit, and headed back to the firepit, where we were all meeting up. We reserved early in the year to get cabins next to each other. The middle cabin became our designated place to gather.

When I got there, Rachel's teenage boy was already trying to start the fire. After a few minutes, he succeeded, quite pleased with himself. The grownups grabbed chairs and placed them around the fire, which became the center of our activities. Vara started barbecuing chicken drumsticks on the grill next to her cabin. Zoe made salads and vegetarian sandwiches. Bowls of chips filled one corner of the table. Kids begged for marshmallows, an annual ritual along with buying marshmallow sticks. Some parents didn't like the idea of using sticks found in the woods because of germs. Rachel opened bottles of red and white wine. Michael preferred a cold can of beer. The fire stoked our appetites. We ate in a circle around the glowing flames. Everyone brought so much food that even after we'd eaten so much, plenty of leftovers remained on the table.

After dinner, we got our sweaters and shawls and settled around the campfire. The kids roasted their marshmallows, while the adults talked into the night. Usually, we started with an update on how we were doing. We started with the typical career updates since none of us worked together anymore. Nick had his own company and had another new business idea to go after. Scott created a new holiday called Singles Day on October 1 to celebrate singleness. Rachel asked everyone how their parents were doing. Then the conversation gravitated to politics, childhood memories, looking up at the stars, and saying how great it felt being outside of the city for a change. At some point, one parent checked the time and told the kids to go to bed. Most didn't want to but didn't put up a fight. My friends had all raised polite kids who listened to them.

Once the kids were gone, Rachel looked around the group and said, "So what do you really want to do in life?" Zoe said she wanted to be a doctor when she was in college and never thought she'd end up working in the software industry. I didn't know that. In fact, I knew her as a project manager since we met at Sapient. Samantha changed her mind several times, getting different Ivy League degrees, which, looking back, she said was not the best use of her time. Vara liked what she was doing as a product manager. Nick wanted to create a travel companion mobile app. Scott, a marketing manager, wrote screenplays and dabbled in writing comedies on the side.

In front of these close friends, I felt comfortable enough to share my own dreams. "If I didn't have to worry about making a living, I'd want to be a full-time writer. I didn't study English or literature, but I really enjoy writing. It makes me feel like I have a special purpose in my life: to share experiences I hope are worth sharing." No one was surprised.

Michael said, "Just do that outside of work."

"You're already doing it," Scott added.

All my girlfriends smiled and nodded at me, having already heard me discuss my dreams during our dinners.

At one point, Scott broke the companionable silence. "We'll need to get more wood tomorrow. We almost used all of it tonight." As the fire died out, we said our quiet goodnights.

I went back to my tiny cabin and took a quick shower. Looking out the window, I noticed the lake reflected moonshine in the middle of the campsite. Bugs occasionally chirped in the peaceful quiet. Satisfied, I let myself fall asleep.

I never used an alarm clock when glamping with my friends. We never imposed a morning meeting time. I woke up around 10 a.m., got dressed, and walked to the central cabin. Most everyone else was already up making breakfast for the kids.

Sometimes there was no need for talking. This particular morning, the wives and I decided to go on a little walk after breakfast. We admired nature, trees, and flowers, enjoyed the cool wind, and listened to the tramping sound we made on the small rocks under our feet. All of our worries and stress from the city were forgotten for a moment.

On Saturday night, the kids wanted to build another fire. All the women announced the various food items they brought with them. Some needed to be cooked; others were taken out of bags and assembled. Magically, a festive dinner appeared again on the picnic table next to the fire. More wine. More beer. More marshmallows. More great talks around the fire.

After a weekend in the woods with two nights in front of the fire, we all packed up by noon on Sunday, hugged each other, and said our goodbyes, while the women made plans to see each other again soon. I felt thankful to get away with my girlfriends and their families for a weekend. At the same time, going home gave me comfort. *I can hear myself again.* I felt content to resume my single life with more books, songs, food, and solo adventures. *I have more time to myself than any of them.* Life went back to being simple again.

As we grew older, it became harder to make glamping happen. I still have photos of all the kids sitting together on a bench from each year. They got bigger and bigger so quickly in front of my eyes. I'm glad we were able to do this for a few years while the children were still small.

For a few years straight, we also continued holding our own annual holiday dinner just for the adults. Michael and the husbands appreciated being included to dine with the women. "You ladies go out for dinner to nice restaurants once a month," Michael said. "Now we're finally invited."

I met Rachel, Michael, and other close friends at college or through work. When we all first met, I didn't know some of us would stay friends for almost three decades. I'd seen my friends through dating and relationships, weddings and births, and job changes. They shared with me the difficulties of meeting someone special, getting pregnant, and taking care of their babies or sick parents. For Rachel and others, working full time and being a mother and wife presented a challenge.

Rachel said once, "Today I just want to run away for an hour and read a book." But she never did. In addition to telling me jokes and stories about her husband and kids, she stood by them day after day.

I, on the other hand, had free time to enjoy. As a treat to myself, I subscribed to the Huntington and Central Square Theater Companies. Each year, they mailed me all the tickets for the season. I marked the dates of the scheduled shows on my calendar—all on Saturday afternoons.

On the day of a matinee, I'd take the appropriate ticket out of a paper envelope and hop on the T. I didn't know anything about the show except for its name. I liked surprises. Also, after having attended shows from these two different theater companies, I knew what kind of productions to expect.

I was one of the first few people inside the Huntington Avenue Theater that particular day and sat in my usual seat. Looking around, I saw only a few people my age; most were older couples or groups. The house lights flashed, signaling the show would soon start, and everyone settled into their seats.

An hour and a half of storytelling and acting ensued, and I was taken to another time and another world. I was amazed by the performances and narrative. The set surprised me, and the dialogue from the stage was loud and clear. I felt at ease and focused my attention completely on the play. During intermission, I people-watched. *What's that couple's life story? Do they always enjoy the theater together?* After the show, I felt recharged and wondered where I should grab a snack. My afternoon adventure continued.

Another hideout of mine was Club Passim in Harvard Square. There, I could hear the clear voice of a singer without any assisted sound effects. Unlike going to the theaters, my concert-going was more spontaneous. Sometimes on a Friday morning, I'd look at the calendar at Passim and buy a ticket for that night. Passim was a small space. After trying different locations, I ended up sitting on the right side of the room. That spot had the best view.

I liked spending time with my friends but also truly enjoyed alone time, preferring live performances over movies or TV shows. Over the years, I occasionally invited Rachel, Michael, or other friends to join me. When they did, it was just a nice bonus.

11

A LOVE NOTE AND FIGHTS

When it came to relationships, my parents—unlike Rachel and Michael—never pressured me to do anything. Even though they were Taiwanese, their parenting style was completely hands off.

My dad once told me when I graduated from Cornell, "You are fully responsible for your own life. So live well." Soon after that, my parents were separated. For years during that time, in moments of anger, my mother shouted, "Let's get a divorce!" Once my dad felt I would be able to take care of myself, he finally gave in to my mother's demands. Every few years, he reminded me about how important it was that I was able to take care of myself.

"I am dating a guy I met online," I told him soon after I started dating at the age of forty-one.

"Be safe. There are many bad people out there."

"Do you want to know what he's like?" *What would Dad want to know?*

"It doesn't matter—as long as you're happy." He was always so supportive.

My parents never asked about dating or men. They also

never told me to get married and have kids. In some ways, they were unusually liberal compared to traditional Taiwanese parents. The rest of my extended family also never hinted that my future might entail being a sad old maid destined to die in loneliness, which my other single female friends heard all the time. I'm thankful my family let me be who I am.

There was only one exception. When I visited my mother's younger sister in Taiwan, she asked if I had met any good men.

"If you were living in Taiwan, I would have done something about you and put this single nonsense to a stop. Your mother is not doing her job." At the time, as a thirty-five-year-old American, I didn't take it to heart, nor was I affected by it. But I remembered her words and my inability to meet that traditional social expectation.

My parents were hands off not only when it came to relationships but about everything else. I believe they were busy trying to survive themselves. After we moved to the United States, Dad, starting with nothing, had to work around the clock and abandon his hobbies like hiking, fishing, photography, and badminton. Mother kept herself in the study most days, trying to follow her academic and professional ambition while fighting schizophrenia. Her need for seclusion had a big impact on her relationship with my father.

In fact, when Rachel first suggested online dating to me, I wondered if my initial hesitation was rooted in what I saw happen with my parents. Their relationship was not a successful one. They'd originally met through my dad's cousin, who was a classmate of my mother and introduced them. Both my parents grew up in large families with seven and eight siblings. They married because their family statuses matched—both upper-middle class. Shortly before their marriage, Dad's parents unexpectedly lost everything they had, and he and his siblings had to make a living on their own, along with supporting their parents. I suspect that's why my parents argued violently with each other for as long as I could remember.

Mother left Dad and me when I was four to study in the Philippines for a couple of years. I don't remember this. I was told that I was being taken care of by my aunts. Then when I was seven, she moved to New York City on her own, and my parents were separated for eight years, living in two different countries. I was always a daddy's girl. Plus my grandparents, along with Uncle Mike and Aunt Christina, moved in with Dad and me. Therefore, I didn't miss her.

When I was fourteen, Dad told me that he had to go to New York. Six months later, my mother came to Taipei to pick me up. Dad left Taipei on Taiwanese Children's Day, and on Taiwan's National Day, I was moved across the sea to the other side of the globe, leaving everyone I loved behind.

Later on, I would learn that Mother was sick with schizophrenia for the first time, and Dad had come to the United States to help her. The trigger might have been the stress from Columbia's PhD program. My mother and I never talked about it. A few years later, I would learn that on the maternal side of my family, there was a history of mental problems never discussed publicly. Growing up, I didn't know that the tendency toward schizophrenia was in my genes.

When the three of us reunited and lived under one roof in New York City and then New Jersey, my parents spent their limited time together arguing, while Dad worked both day and night shifts at a food factory as a mechanical engineer looking after machines. Mother, a proud academic, buried her head in books as she continued to pursue her PhD at Columbia University. During high school, I saw her oscillate between holding a job and studying for her PhD, as well as getting sick, then better, and then relapsing over and over again. On the other hand, Dad was a handyman, down to earth, practical, and hardworking. Yet there was something about him that Mother remained unhappy about. I was too young to understand their arguments. I thought they might have avoided each other unconsciously. Since they were so volatile when they were together, I preferred when they didn't see each other. I stayed out of sight, kept my head in my schoolwork, and hung out with my friends.

Soon after I turned eighteen, Dad drove me to Ithaca, and I spent the next four and a half years happily at Cornell. When I graduated from college and moved into my own apartment, they finally decided to separate. It was as if they no longer had to stay together for my benefit. I felt relieved. Their relationship was chaotic, combative, and hard.

I remember the first boy I liked, Lee-Chi. I was maybe six or seven. He was in my first-grade class. Back then, in Taiwan, children were seated based on height. Lee-Chi and I were the same height, and both of us sat in the last row in the back of the classroom. I'm not able to say now why I liked him. Perhaps it was just chemistry or proximity at school. During recess, the whole class ran out of the classroom. I could always spot him. Once I found him, I'd chase him around the schoolyard, passing noisy monkeys, beautiful peacocks, and colorful birds. Once I reached him—poor boy for being liked—I hit him, which was the only time I hit someone in my life. We both laughed. Then I chased him all over again until the school bell rang, telling us to go back to the classroom. I never got tired of this in first grade.

But that boisterous little girl was not the same once we moved to the United States. Twelve years later, at Cornell, I slowly broke out of my reserved, immigrant shell, having lived in America for four years. Cornell was a big place with many interesting people. Like all the other bright-eyed freshmen, I was excited to meet new friends. One of the things I found attractive about Cornell was its size. I'd never run out of people to meet.

One day, early in my first semester of freshman year, I noticed a group of guys who often hung out together. During dinner at our dining hall, I'd often go out of my way to say hi to them; in fact, I found excuses to go over to them. I didn't know how to do more than say hello, so nothing ever came of it. That year, one boy from my engineering classes stood out to me. He appeared friendly and smart, was always smiling, and always aced his exams. I developed a crush on him. Every time I saw him on campus, my heart raced. One night, I asked him to meet up.

"What's up?" He gazed down at me as the two of us stood in an empty hallway.

I had written a love note and gave it to him. He opened the paper and read it: "I think you are a great guy. I like you a lot. I am not sure what to do about that. Just want to let you know that's how I feel."

I watched him attentively. All of a sudden, he got all red. He pulled his cap lower to cover his face. He didn't know how to respond. Finally, he said, "Thank you."

Then we hurriedly parted, both embarrassed. I went back

to my dorm room and hid under my blanket for who knows how long. The only thing I knew how to do was write a note.

Still, we stayed friendly toward each other. A few weeks later, he made a tape with his favorite songs for me, though he hadn't said that he liked me back. I learned every song. I felt happy that I'd paid him the highest compliment I knew. But we just remained friends. Years later, he ended up with a girlfriend whom I knew. She was nice. I was glad they seemed happy because, by that time, I'd grown out of the crush I had on him. I realized that he'd received my one and only love note, scribbled with a regular pen on a small piece of plain white paper, and, to my horror now, it had not been spell-checked.

My understanding of an ideal life started with my big family in Taiwan when I was a child at the age of four, living with and watching my grandparents, Dad, Aunt Theresa, Uncle Mike, and Aunt Christina—all under one roof—while my mother was away in the United States. My grandparents had seven children: five sons and two daughters. I lived with three of them, who were unmarried at the time, plus Dad. My father's two other younger brothers, Uncle Jeff and Uncle Frasier, were both married already. Their sons, my cousins, Calvin and Jimmy, also lived with us. On weekends and holidays, we were always all together, eating, laughing, going out, and spending time with each other. I felt loved by all the adults. Unlike the way my mother acted toward me as a young child, no one yelled at or hit me.

In my teens in the United States, Dad and Mother showed me what could go wrong. Not every relationship was happy and wonderful. That's when I understood that being alone could be better than being with the wrong person. Then with Oliver and Chris, my first serious relationships at age twenty and twenty-two, I experienced unconditional love. I had many happy moments with both of them. I believed I was lucky to have them in my life at such a young age.

Perhaps due to my Taiwanese-ness, thinking about karma, I told myself I might have used up all my good fortune, and I shouldn't be greedy and ask for more when it came to relationships.

12

SLEEPING UNDER THE STARS

At the age of twenty-eight, after I lost Chris and my first job, travel came to the rescue. I'd never planned a trip myself, and this would be the perfect time to do it. I had no responsibilities to a job or to any person, and I had enough savings to take a break for six months. Inside me existed a deep curiosity about the rest of the world. Because I'd experienced life in Taipei, New York City, a New Jersey suburb, and Boston, I knew there were endless other cities to explore, people from different backgrounds and cultures to meet, and cuisines with unique local ingredients to try.

Travel became an important personal goal, and I wanted to make sure it happened. I started looking for a European tour and talked to everyone I knew, not sure if I needed a travel partner and how I would do it safely. Carey, whom I'd never met but was the girlfriend of my college friend Matt from Vancouver, expressed interest in accompanying me when I mentioned this to him. She suggested the Contiki tour company that targeted travelers ages eighteen to thirty-five, as well as

its European Whirlpool tour. Since I'd only been to Barcelona with Chris, I was up to going anywhere in Europe. I was
excited to have a travel partner who had done all the research
already. We decided on the dates and picked an itinerary over
email. I packed, not sure how much stuff I needed to bring.
But whatever it was, everything had to fit into a medium-sized
suitcase that I'd bought just for the trip. We couldn't wait to
leave. It was my very first big trip without Chris.

I told my friends and the handful of former teachers I kept
in touch with about my European travel plans. One of my
middle-school teachers told me it would be like a coming-out
trip for prestigious children in America in olden times. She
wished me a wonderful vacation.

On April 16, 2002, I excitedly boarded a Virgin Atlantic
flight from Boston to London's Heathrow Airport and met
Carey at the hotel meeting place for our tour. She was my
height and build with a more angular face, an Asian born in
Canada. We smiled at each other, excited to get going.

We were joined by about twenty other young travelers
from America, Australia, Canada, and Japan. Our tour guide
was an energetic, handsome man who looked my age or
perhaps a few years younger. Our bus driver appeared to be
a quieter man but equally nice. All of us packed into the tour
bus. Our itinerary included London, Amsterdam, Munich,
Mauthausen, Vienna, Venice, Rome, Florence, Interlaken
and Lauterbrunnen, Paris, and then back to London—all in
eighteen days. From London to Amsterdam, we took a ferry
across the North Sea. The tour motto was "We are here for a
good time, not a long time."

Every time we arrived in a new city, the tour guide handed
out a city map marked with places of interest. Luckily, Carey

and I were both map people. We'd quickly compare what we wanted to see, and as soon as the tour guide dismissed us, we'd sprint into the city crowds together.

The architecture in Europe was nothing like anything I'd ever seen. Churches everywhere. Tulips, wooden shoes, and the red-light district in Amsterdam. Large steins of beer in Munich. The gold Mozart statue and Mozart chocolates in Vienna. Canals and a gondola ride in Venice. The Pantheon, Colosseum, Trevi Fountain, and Vatican City in Rome. The famed David statue in Florence. The lion monument and wooden cabins in Lucerne. The Eiffel Tower, Notre Dame, and Arch of Triumph in Paris. And more churches. We packed in as much as possible.

In the past, when I traveled with Chris, I collected different souvenirs such as bells or small ceramic figures, which were breakable, hard to store, and didn't really make me happy later. On this trip, I ended up buying magnets from each city, which were cheap and small, and silver rings, which were also small and something I could wear when I got home. Collecting magnets and rings to remember my trips became travel traditions that I still honor today.

I'd not thought about Chris since leaving Logan Airport. I loved living out of a suitcase and seeing Europe at hyper speed. I felt a new kind of history coming alive in front of me as I walked through all kinds of streets—not American or Taiwanese. I felt energized and alive again!

I took a chance traveling with Carey, and it worked out wonderfully. She was easy to spend time with. While some younger people on the tour wanted to hit every single bar in the cities we were visiting for 1 p.m. beer runs, Carey and I wanted to explore the cities, walk with the locals, and see as many notable churches, markets, and stores as possible. We were laidback and flexible with each other. Perhaps the only difference between us was that I was curious about other travelers and sometimes struck up conversations with them, while Carey preferred to keep to ourselves.

On the flight back to Boston from London, I couldn't stop looking through all the pictures on my Sony digital camera. I'd never taken so many all at once. I wanted to capture every moment. Every one of my senses had experienced something fresh. Since that trip, there has forever been a travel bug in me. When I returned to Boston in May, I was very much recharged and felt like I had the freedom to do anything I wanted.

I decided to see a new city every year. I was opportunistic about traveling and planned my own trips. At the age of thirty-four, six years after the European Whirlpool tour, I took one of my favorite trips. Out of the blue, Rachel offered a great idea: "Mary and I are thinking about going to Greece. Do you want to come?" Of course, I said yes. After three or four email exchanges, the three of us booked our tickets to Athens. We made quick decisions—just like how we worked. Our first stop was Santorini. We took a ferry from Athens. Water transportation in the Aegean was easy to navigate. Our ferry carried passengers, bikes, cars, and trucks. The port we left from was as organized as an airport, handling multiple ferries docking and leaving on different schedules.

My first impression of Santorini came from the back of the ship underneath the passenger compartment while the boat slowly opened its door to a wall of rock. Just rock! Then my face was greeted with dust from the island.

The second impression was seeing a huge crowd of people rushing off the ferry, not knowing which way to go.

A taxi driver refused to take us to our hotel. People yelled and scrambled off in all different directions. Eventually, we persuaded a driver to cram us into his small bus, along with eight other visitors.

Going from the port up to the center of town to our hotel, the bus drove the same way one would ski down a black diamond trail: on a forty-five-degree hill, from side to side, with quick turns to stay on course—except we were on a bus. I was scared and amazed at the skill of the bus driver. We kept going higher and higher, and the water became farther away.

In the part of the world that I knew, people built their homes on flat land. In Santorini, they ignored the easy choice and lived mostly on the steep side facing a volcano, getting a fantastic view of the ocean. This made stairs a necessity of life. From the door of our hotel to our room, we went down at least thirty steps, pulling our luggage with their useless wheels.

Unlike a city trying to secure its place in the world, Santorini was content with its own culture and style. Skyscrapers did not exist. As if it had snowed both indoors and outdoors, all the houses—their roofs, walls, furniture, sheets, and towels—were covered in white. Against the glaring white, the deep-blue colors of the sky and the glowing yellow sun were sprinkled in.

Santorini, a global destination, drew people from all over the world. We danced with all varieties of singles—Austrians, Canadians, Americans, and French—and got free drinks from a flirtatious Athenian bartender until the bar closed. We did all that we could during the day, walking through Fira and Oia, checking out shops and restaurants, trying out crepes and ice cream, looking at artwork, watching the sunset, and searching for a shooting star. We could not compete, however, with the local women when it came to heels: beautiful women walking in three-inch high heels on stone-paved, hilly paths with steps going up and down. Instead of stretching what our feet could do, we focused on stretching our stomachs. We tasted as much food as we could, sharing all the dishes and eating in small portions. Unlike my experience with Bostonian Greek food, I was pleasantly surprised by authentic, tasty, and light Greek food. Greek salad in Greece is definitely better than what we have at home.

One of my girlfriends in Boston had been excited about my opportunity to meet singles from across the ocean. *What happens if I do meet someone I like here? What would I do? Move away for him? Or would he move from his homeland to be with me?*

Santorini was an island of white and blue, fine cuisine and artwork, tradition and tourist attractions. I wished I could stay longer—perhaps it was the islander in me that was calling out—but I knew the ship leaving Santorini would be on time.

A few days before we left, Rachel had intriguing news. "My friend George might be able to take us on a sailing trip if he's in town. He'll contact me and let me know today." She later got the call that he could take us for a sail.

George and his dad, plus the three of us, boarded their boat. George planned the whole trip. We visited three islands frequented only by locals. We lived on the water for three blissful days. I saw the most amazing sunrise on the water, the whitest sand beach, and the most turquoise seawater. Similar to the openness and blueness that I saw when I was on a cruise with Chris to the Caribbean, I fell in love with everything about sailing in Greece.

There was no traffic, and there were no roads to follow. We

were free to go wherever we wanted. Sailing felt like absolute freedom and adventure. As soon as we left the shore, I was drawn to the front of the ship and left my girlfriends in the back. I felt so peaceful and content sitting there, just watching everything go by.

The boat might have been small, but it had everything one needed to survive. I learned to use the manual toilet and took a shower in the stern out in the open while wearing my bikini. For food, George made a fresh salad for lunch, which we all enjoyed. At night, we docked the boat and visited local restaurants for yummy meals.

When I got up one morning, George said, "The best way to wake up is to jump into the sea." I thought, *Hey, why not?* So I jumped in. The water felt warm and wonderful.

On the second night, when we were all ready for bed, George said, "If you want, you can sleep on the top under the stars." I loved that. So I didn't sleep in my bunk but on top of the seating area. Amazingly enough, the next morning, I was awakened by a small ray of sunlight that got brighter and larger. I sat up and saw the sunrise while the boat rocked slightly back and forth.

For the first time in a long while, I thought, *I wouldn't mind meeting someone like George.* He was cute, kind, smart, and adventurous. I admit I had a bit of a harmless crush on him, but I knew nothing could develop between us since he lived in Athens and had a beautiful girlfriend who was a pilot.

I absolutely loved sailing. Part of me felt a desire to be a nomad and global citizen. When I came home, I even considered buying a boat. *Could I live on a boat?* A boat was not cheap, and you needed a slip or mooring in the harbor—also not cheap. A boat wouldn't have a modern bathroom. Plus, I had tons of stuff and wasn't good at swimming. Boston had harsh winters, which meant that I couldn't live on a boat there all year round. Thinking about it practically and realistically, I obviously couldn't live on a boat. But I was learning about myself, what worked for me for a few days of vacation and what I needed every day. I promised myself I'd take another sailing trip when the opportunity arose.

When no friends were available to travel with me, I went abroad on my own—usually joining a tour group so that I wasn't entirely alone. Most of the tours were filled with retired couples, but I didn't feel left out, and I met many other like-minded travelers. I met retirees who were spending their time traveling the world after working hard and raising families. "Hi! Come sit with us." The couples from the trip would invite me to join them during lunch or dinner. "We love the company." Occasionally, I also met single women traveling alone. "I checked with the tour company to make sure there were younger people on the trip, and they told me about you," a single young woman said. I tried to learn about the travelers I crossed paths with. *How did they come to this point in their lives? Why are they traveling? Where are they from? What do they do for a living?* One couple told me, "It's great that you're traveling so young. We had to wait until we were retired. We wish we could have started earlier." I became good friends with some of them and keep in touch to this day.

Since my first trip to Europe with Carey, I've traveled to many incredible places in this world. When standing on top of Machu Picchu, I was amazed by the ancient architecture. How did they move all the rocks on top of the mountain and build this sophisticated place? Our tour group took the train and the bus up the mountain. I climbed from the gate to the top, having to stop many times and feeling quite out of shape. The view on top was breathtaking and totally worth the climb. The ancient Incas built rooms for worship, classrooms, storage, living quarters, and an area for farming, all surrounded by other mountain peaks and low, wandering clouds.

When visiting the major cities in Europe, I was impressed with the history visible in every corner. Unlike other places I visited, Iceland preserved its majestic waterfalls and geysers. I didn't want to stop soaking in the Blue Lagoon. I had dinners on a boat restaurant in La Seine overlooking Notre Dame and on a floating restaurant in the canal in Venice. I'd seen the Mona Lisa and gloried inside the Forbidden City. I compared the beaches in the Caribbean to those in Greece. I'd also seen kids begging and selling things in Acapulco, Cusco, and Beijing. Homeless people wandered about some of the more hidden streets. In Austria, filled with emotion, I stood in the Mauthausen concentration camp. Everywhere I went, the local tour guides and bus drivers loved and were proud of their countries.

My life goal is to visit all the continents at least once and add to my collection of eighty-three magnets. I once told a friend, "I want to go to Africa." He was from Tanzania and laughed, saying, "Well, you might have to pick something smaller. Africa is pretty big." I knew I had much more to learn about the world.

When I travel, I feel something bigger than myself, and I stop worrying about the little stuff. I find diversity, hospitality, history, and culture. I see decadence and poverty. Every trip, no matter how short or long, is a reset and recharge. Each trip home provides me with the ability to reflect on how to live my life better. My mental space expands. I hope to continue to learn about the world and see beyond myself.

13

SINGLE MOTHER BY CHOICE

In 2010, when I turned thirty-six, I heard my biological clock ticking as I sat in the living room of my Back Bay apartment. The sun streamed in from the bay window, the sky a clear blue. I wanted to have a baby. On my own. All of a sudden, the way I lived my life felt selfish. I wanted to be responsible for more than just me. I wanted to be a mother and imagined a little, moldable person in my life. I pictured taking someone to school, reading books at bedtime, and singing the alphabet song together. I imagined hearing baby talk similar to what I heard from Rachel's adorable and talkative child. I'd always been good at babysitting kids. Not dating anyone or being married wouldn't get in the way of what I wanted.

"I am thinking about starting a family on my own. I want to try to get pregnant," I told my primary care doctor after briefly sitting in the waiting area of Massachusetts General Hospital (MGH) Downtown. Even though the small room was not decorated, it was functional and familiar to me. During my appointment, I sat on the examining table with my legs dangling. I hoped to get Dr. Holbert's advice. She turned around from the computer at the corner of the room and faced me. She didn't change her kind expression after hearing my request. She told me about an organization called Single Mother by Choice (SMBC), which had helpful information for single women deciding to have children.

"They should have a local chapter in Boston," she said. I told her I was still thinking it through. I had more questions about how to go about it and who else I should talk to. My doctor knew what else was on my mind. "Also, look into the New England Cryogenic Center," she said, which was a place where I could purchase donor sperm. "If you decide to proceed, you can call a fertility doctor. I recommend Dr. Charles Smith at the women's clinic in Alewife. Since you don't have fertility issues, he should be able to help you with the procedure." I appreciated her direct manner backed by knowledge. It was easy to talk to her about my personal wishes, and she understood what I needed to do.

I looked up SMBC and found their mission statement. It sounded just like me:

> A single mother by choice is a woman who *decides* to have or adopt a child, knowing she would be her child's sole parent, at least at the outset. Typically, we are career women in our thirties and forties. The ticking of our biological clocks has made us face the fact that we can no longer wait for marriage before starting our families. Some of us went to a doctor for donor insemination or adopted in the United States or abroad. Others accidentally became pregnant and discovered we were thrilled. Most of us would have preferred to bring a child into the world with two loving parents, but although we have a lifetime to

marry or find a partner, nature is not as generous in allotting childbearing years.

I signed up for a membership immediately and read through all their articles, discussion forums, and success stories. There were many women considering and doing what I wanted to do.

The next person I consulted was Dr. Han, my psychiatrist. At the time, my primary care doctor (Dr. Holbert) and Dr. Han were not connected in any way; I was managing my physical health separately and independently of my mental health. My appointments with Dr. Han were never more than ten minutes tops—a quick check on my meds and how I was doing. On my next scheduled appointment day, I arrived on time and sat in a long hallway in a stiff chair outside of his office, waiting for about half an hour. He opened his office door, letting someone out and me in. I walked to the square table in the middle of the room, where we always sat on either side, facing each other, and told him what I hoped to do.

"Okay. That should be fine," he said. I was amazed at this simple and easy answer as we sat in the midst of all these papers, documents, binders, and books in his office, covering all the walls and any flat surfaces.

"What about my medication? Is that going to be a problem?" I took Zyprexa for schizophrenia and had been doing so for six years. I'd read online that any medication I took could be passed on to the baby through my bloodstream. I didn't know if my medication was risky or unhealthy for a fetus.

"You can stop taking your medication. If something happens and you need it, you can always start taking it again."

Dr. Han apparently didn't think there was any problem. This was another short appointment. I got up from the chair, said thank you, and walked out of his office. I had official approval from my psychiatrist to stop taking my medication. I felt better. Nothing would be passed on undesirably. Dr. Han didn't try to be more helpful, nor was he proactively playing out worst-case scenarios. *If my mother could have me, I can have a baby,* I figured.

I stopped taking my medication cold turkey. Later on, Rachel would tell me that I should have weaned off it gradually. I had no idea. She couldn't quite believe how little Dr. Han did for me.

When I got home, I called the cryogenic center as my primary care doctor suggested. I looked up their website on my computer beforehand and saw terms like "helpful advice," "caring specialists," and "advanced technology." I read through their services: choosing a donor through a donor catalogue, sperm banking, shipping, and storage. I made sure to make this call at home, where I could talk freely.

A woman answered cheerfully. It took me a second to respond because I felt slightly embarrassed. "I'm looking to start a family on my own. I'm interested in finding someone … a donor." I didn't want to say "sperm."

"Great. We can definitely help you. You can create an account online and review the profiles of our donors. Then when you have made your selection, call us back, and we can help you with your order."

Sounded like a straightforward process. Everything could be done online. No need for in-person appointments or any complicated checkups. I could do this. No problem.

I spent the next six months talking to friends and family.

Comfortable with the idea of being a single mom, I knew it was a big decision—a life-changing one that would affect both me and a child for the rest of our lives. So I wanted to learn as much as I could about being a single mother before it happened. I had many conversations. I talked to married men and women, parents and non-parents, single mothers, single friends, and my family. Most people were supportive and optimistic, but everyone told me that life as I knew it would change forever, and I should go ahead with my plan cautiously.

One father told me to think twice—to "double make sure" this was really what I wanted to do. He even suggested I leave the idea behind for a few weeks and even months and then see if it was still important to me.

A married woman older than I am had been trying to get pregnant for a year at the time, but it had been difficult. The process she and her husband were going through sounded very demanding. There were many doctor appointments and many failed attempts. She prepared me for the worst-case scenario. What a shock for me to learn that at thirty-six, I was already considered old when it came to having a baby. *There is a possibility my body won't easily get pregnant even though I'm healthy and still young at heart.*

A mother I knew thought single motherhood was a good option for me since I hadn't found the right person with whom to have children. There were so many different kinds of families now, and in an area as cosmopolitan and progressive as Boston, being a single mother wouldn't be out of the ordinary. Since I was choosing to be a single mother from the start, I wouldn't struggle in the same way as other women who become single mothers by accident due to the death of a spouse or divorce.

A few married women laughed and said, "You won't need to negotiate with anyone about how to parent your kid."

Some of my friends introduced me to their friends who were single mothers. These women were all creative and driven. One SMBC woman got pregnant through a donor. She also mentioned the SMBC organization to me and said people she'd met online were helpful throughout her journey. She was successful and now had a baby daughter. She said giving birth to her baby was the best thing she'd done in life. When she went to parties now, she would bring the baby along. None of her friends minded. The baby was also very cooperative; she never made much fuss at the adult get-togethers. A divorced mother I met hadn't planned to raise a baby on her own, but after a year, her marriage didn't work out, and she ended up taking care of her baby girl on her own. She rented a small place and joined a single-mother community. She exchanged outgrown baby clothes with other moms. She traded babysitting with them. These mothers figured out how to balance their work and social lives with their babies' needs. They all had this can-do attitude. No one complained. Single mothers are resourceful!

A father told me everything I knew about life would no longer apply once a kid arrived. Still another dad I was friends with explained how his mindset changed after his baby was born. He said my life would no longer be centered around my own plans and schedule. It would be all about the baby. I'd have to fit my needs into the baby's routine. Life as a single person versus life as a single mother represented two opposite ends of living.

I was ready to make changes to my life. I could deal with no personal travel due to not having extra money on a single income and no business travel because I'd need to find extra childcare. Not going out to eat all the time meant saving money; possibly giving up my apartment in the city for a bigger but cheaper place was also quite doable. My mommy friends told me it was okay not to move out of my small one-bedroom place at first. The real test came when looking at photographs with a couple of friends who were taking a year off to travel the world. They shared pictures from Tanzania, which looked amazing. But I didn't feel the desire to go. I was satisfied with staying where I was. I thought my reaction was encouraging and showed I was ready for what I wanted to do.

I spent a weekend printing out the travel photos I loved and posted them on my wall. I could enjoy just looking at where I had been. I thought I should start saving money for the baby. I could also clean the condo and free up more space. I didn't want to act too early or too quickly, but I started to prepare myself for a different life, both mentally and physically.

Another friend shared his personal reflection on being a father of two daughters. "You figure it out as you go. Just when you think you've nailed it, the kids get bigger, and you have to deal with something entirely different. You will never be one hundred percent prepared to be a parent." *Okay, so I can only prepare myself for so much. That's good to know. All I can do is my best.*

The conversations I had with my divorced parents were brief, even though I'd never talked about having a baby before. As I've said, I did not have traditional Taiwanese parents. I'd never received any pressure to have children to pass on our bloodline. They also never expressed any disappointment about not being grandparents. Now that I wanted a baby, they again didn't voice opinions. I remembered the day I called Dad around 6 p.m. on a workday—the usual time I called him—to tell him the news. I caught him just as he arrived home. When I told him I wanted to have a baby alone, he said, "Great! Go for it. As long as you're happy." This was very typical of my dad, who had been supportive of all my life decisions. He believed that as long as I thought through what I wanted to do, I'd be okay.

I didn't usually call my mother since we were not close, and I was fairly independent. When I called and told her my plans, she was very surprised. A few days later, she called back and asked, "How are you going to pay for this?" So typical of her. Then she surprised me by offering to provide financial support if I did have a child. I was touched by this offer and thanked her.

Financially, I believed I could make it work on my own. I had the means to raise a child on one income—a huge advantage over many single mothers. I did some rough calculations, taking into consideration monthly daycare, food, and clothes. If I went ahead with getting pregnant, I planned to put together a budget spreadsheet and start tightening my spending.

Many of my married male friends expressed concern about my chances of meeting a partner in the future. I was not worried about decreasing these chances. Meeting someone was never really something I felt I had to do. Besides, if having a child was a problem for any boyfriend, he was not for me.

Another girlfriend mentioned that as she and her husband got older, they really recognized how fast their children grew up. She wanted to enjoy the brief time when their children still lived at home. *Yes,* I thought. *This is a fifteen- to twenty-year commitment. After that, the child becomes an adult and lives his or her own life.*

I felt that my biggest challenge would be a good support

network. At some point, I'd have to rely more on nearby friends than out-of-state family. My parents lived five hours away. I'd need to come up with tricks. I wondered, *How will I take a shower?* I'd need to find a local community or make my own. I could ask friends for their old baby clothes. I could research daycare options in the area. I could trade childcare with other single mothers. I was sure I could learn more from other mothers. I didn't know everything, but I was willing to learn.

An older woman who had remarried and only had step-children told me, "This is a decision you and only you can make for yourself. I can only tell you that I wish I'd had children of my own."

Another single woman my age said, "I don't understand why you want to do this on your own. Life will be so difficult. You should meet someone and have a partner to have kids with." She sounded like me before I'd had the thought of becoming an SMBC. *Yes, life will be different, but I am ready. I want to be a mom.* I responded to her, "I don't think life will be so hard. I can handle it. I'm up for the challenge." My friend didn't push me further on this. In the end, she just smiled and left me alone.

In some ways, speaking to my friends openly about the idea of becoming an SMBC was a good test for me. *Can I continue on the path toward starting a family with all the support, encouragement, questions, and objections around me? Am I strong enough to have more of these conversations?* I thought that in the process of becoming an SMBC, I might lose a friend or two who honestly didn't understand or agree with my decisions and actions. But, ultimately, I felt good about going ahead with trying to get pregnant.

In August 2010, four to five months after the thought

of single motherhood had first entered my mind, I emailed Rachel about my first milestone: "Ordered!" I wrote excitedly and continued:

> I picked someone. I finally ordered the "stuff" I need for the first try. Feeling good about it. There's a lot more drama in reading through long profiles for each person (seventeen pages) and debating different aspects of these data than in selecting one. I got my primary doctor involved as well. Googling medical information online is really dangerous. The information online is large in volume and is also in pieces. Just called the doctor's office to get confirmation they received the stuff. I think at the end of August, I should be doing my first try! Pretty happy. But also don't want to be prematurely happy.

I'd called the New England Cryogenic Center (NECC) and ordered four vials of donor D#### for $2,010, including shipping. One day later, the vials were couriered to Dr. Smith at the women's clinic in Alewife. The baby plan was now more than just talk. I might be able to do the intrauterine insemination in August.

Rachel wrote back in a few minutes: "OMG, that's so exciting. How did you make the final pick? Congrats! And good luck! Let us know how it goes."

For the past couple of months, I'd been looking through the donor catalogue, trying to figure out how to select a donor. The first time I looked at the list, I was very much overwhelmed. I closed the web browser after one minute. The second time I looked at the list, I was prepared with my own Excel spreadsheet. I checked through more than one hundred profiles one by one, reading each person's short bio. I categorized each donor on my spreadsheet and eliminated anyone who was married, had allergies, would release his ID in the future, and might have a religious preference—I didn't want anyone who might want to get involved with my baby later or would want me to bring up the baby with any kind of religious practice.

I talked openly with Rachel about the donors, including sharing with her the long profiles I'd purchased for ten dollars each. No donor name was given, just a letter and a few numbers. There were no pictures, only descriptions of physical traits, personal characteristics, fertility history, and personal and family health histories.

The first donor who caught my attention was B###, or Swedish, as I called him. Knowing many happy interracial couples, I wanted diversity in my child's genes. I had recently attended a Finnish friend's baby shower, and all the Finnish women I'd met seemed talented and genuine. They'd made amazing-looking, tasty desserts. They talked about how they stayed in touch and got together regularly. They seemed to care deeply for each other, catching up on the latest family updates. Nordic heritage impressed me, so perhaps this was the guy.

The second donor of interest was D###, or "the writer." He listed five different European countries as part of his heritage. I liked that a lot. I wanted someone who was multicultural, and I indirectly assumed he was. His seventeen-page profile looked perfect. I sent it to Rachel to discuss. She commented that the writer had interesting things to say, a definite improvement over the Swedish profile, which felt less multicultural. The second donor sounded capable of more personal insight. I also imagined he might be logical as well as creative. Therefore, his child might inherit those same equally important qualities. Perfect—almost. There was one odd thing in the profile: sugar in his urine. I called NECC, and the receptionist informed me her lab director said his numbers for that were perfectly normal. That happens in some people. It's genetic.

Without eliminating the writer, I looked into a third person in more detail, which meant I bought his long profile too. D####, or "the smart guy," listed himself as a chemistry graduate student at Harvard. His SAT scores were high, except he was taking Trazodone. I looked it up, and Google results showed it was an antidepressant. With my mental health history as well as my mother's genes, I thought having more mental health issues in my baby's family line could be a bad move. But this guy sounded very solid. Nothing unusual or unhealthy.

It was down to the writer or smart guy. I Googled for more info on both concerns and did not find any useful information. Then I emailed my doctor, who gave me her take. She did not think that having sugar was normal and said that Trazodone was now used more as a sleep aid. She suggested I should find out more about why that person took that medicine.

I also asked another doctor friend about this to get one more opinion. He reminded me that having a parent who went to Harvard does not mean their kid is going to go to Harvard. Good point!

Even though I had detailed medical information on each donor, it still felt like I needed to know more. From my perspective, this was a decision about biology and genetics. I was doing my best to make the right choice based on the information I had on paper, not from a man standing in front of me. I decided not to focus on issues that were not there but instead do the best that I could and know how to do it.

I called NECC and asked my questions: "Was there any test specifically done to rule out diabetes for the writer?" It had been a generic urine test. Again, I was told the sugar was nothing to worry about. I asked why the other donor was taking Trazodone and was told that it was to help with sleep. He took it for a while and did not like the drug, so he stopped.

I felt it was risky to go with the writer with sugar. That felt like a big unknown. I'm aware that one's concept of "big" is relative, and I kept reminding myself there were another seventeen pages of good stuff. In the end, I decided to pick the smart guy.

While reviewing the donor profiles, I also made an appointment with Dr. Smith's office. A nurse met with me and explained in detail what I needed to do. "We will perform intra-uterine insemination (IUI) every month during the time of your ovulation. Since you don't have any known fertility issues, we can start with IUI. You can consider in vitro fertilization (IVF) later if we're not successful." I made a mental note to Google "IUI" and "IVF."

She continued, "You'll have to start tracking your basal body temperature (BBT) every day so you can see the increase in your temperature, which indicates that you've ovulated or are in your most fertile days. Here's a blank chart you can keep next to your bed. Of course, you can also get an over-the-counter ovulation predictor kit (OPK). You can find them at CVS." I looked at the paper she'd just handed me with all the lines on it, thinking, *Gotta go to CVS.*

She went on. "On the day you see an increase in your BBT or when the OPK turns, indicating ovulation, and when you're ready, call the office between nine and nine fifteen in the morning to let us know you want to come in. We'll confirm the schedule for that day. The IUI will be performed two days in a row to increase the chances of getting you pregnant. The last thing," she said, "is you can store your tanks here."

"Tanks?"

"Sperm. You will need two tanks per month, one for each IUI."

"Oh, got it. Great."

"Once you're pregnant, you can continue to see Dr. Smith until your midterm. We can discuss that more when the time comes."

I walked out of the women's clinic feeling I had a solid understanding of the plan. The whole process sounded pretty natural to me, but it had to be the right time. Once a vial of sperm was injected into me, a single sperm still had to do the work and get to my egg. It was human biology.

With the knowledge of what needed to be done, I had to decide how many vials to buy. How many tries did I need? I had to get enough vials for me to have sufficient attempts to get to a successful pregnancy. If I didn't have the appropriate number of vials to get pregnant, and the supply for this particular donor ran out, I'd need to start the research again and use a different donor. Would I want more than one baby? And if so, did I want them to be from the same donor? I didn't think I could plan that far ahead. Most likely, I'd have one child. It might be all I could handle by myself.

I also had to decide if I wanted to give the child the option to find out who the donor was when he or she became of legal age. My child might have half-siblings somewhere in the world. I thought I'd allow it if the child asked.

Plus, there was the cost of a vial to consider, which was a

significant matter to ponder. I decided on four: two tries for two months.

Decisions made. A small step forward. Now I had to wait for my period to start the BBT charting process.

My best friend from high school, who had a son, thought my email, "Ordered," meant that I had ordered something online for my friends. Once she realized what I was talking about, she was happy for me. She said maybe I should skip breakfasts now so that I would get a girl. She had definitely voted for a girl! "Take folic acid. Sleep and eat well. Prepare your body. And, hopefully, you won't have to try too many times!" *I can definitely do all that,* I thought. But I didn't specifically want a girl since a boy or a girl is equally a blessing. A few of my friends who were moms wanted to celebrate with me. I wasn't ready to celebrate yet since I knew there were so many more steps I had to go through and factors that could affect the outcome. But I was happy they were excited for me.

In June 2010, I started tracking and charting my BBT on a spreadsheet. I went to CVS and bought a specific thermometer for this; a basal thermometer was more precise than a normal one. I also bought three different brands of ovulation tests. I wanted to be sure. This was probably the longest time I'd ever spent in CVS. Based on my friend's suggestion, I also bought a bottle of folic acid.

I placed the thermometer and chart on my bedside table. Every morning when I woke up, I measured my resting temperature. During the first month, I gathered data. In addition to tracking the old-fashioned way by taking my own temperature, I also peed in a cup and dipped in digital ovulation test sticks I'd found at CVS. It was very similar to how women test to see if they're pregnant. These tests would tell me if I was on one of my two most fertile days. Since one of the tests was cheaper, I took that test every day after my period ended. Then it got close to the probable dates. I took all three kinds of tests to see the results and how they compared to the temperature curve. Luckily, modern science worked, and everything made sense. I continued with month two. Having multiple ways of tracking and crosschecking made me feel more confident about being able to identify my most fertile day of the month.

When I had two months of data, I had enough to predict when my next ovulation would be. I found a few online websites and mobile apps that helped me log information and predict the next cycle. I was using all the tools I was told to use. It felt like a science project. I thought I would be ready for my first IUI in August.

During the process, my friend and ex-boyfriend Oliver spoke out strongly against my plan, telling me this was not a good idea. This came from a caring and logical person I'd known since college; he was also a medical doctor who'd successfully planned everything out in his life. He was happily married with two children. And he knew I had schizophrenia.

Unlike my relationship with Chris, which was known by all my friends in Boston, only my college friends knew Oliver. He was my first boyfriend ever. He was also Taiwanese, tall, smart, and caring. Like me, he was born in Taiwan, went to high school in the Dominican Republic, and attended Cornell for college.

He had given me so much love since day one. He never hesitated to look me in the eyes and say, "I want to build a life with you together." Oliver was one of those boyfriends who read self-help books on dating and relationships and followed the advice. He was the perfect person to have as a first boyfriend. After learning that my favorite flowers were tulips, he often brought me dozens of them. They were my first times receiving flowers from a man. He dedicated Celine Dion's song "Because You Loved Me" to us, which I listened to on repeat. I learned how to kiss and make love with him. Oliver created my first idea of a boyfriend, and he had set a high bar.

With his glasses and slightly untamed hair, he looked like a geek, in a good way. He had graduated from Cornell two years ahead of me. After he graduated and went to medical school, we continued our relationship long distance. We talked on the phone often. In my diary, I noted, "Today I had the courage to tell him what was on my mind." I remember I disagreed with him on what I should read. He had left me some of his old books, but I wasn't interested in reading them. He thought I could improve my mind. Sometimes I was amazed how Tim, his older brother, and Oliver would openly debate certain topics. That was not something I grew up with, a sibling to debate with. I preferred listening.

As a twenty-year-old, I felt pressured by such a mature man. At the end of our long-distance relationship, I wavered. I was too young to be so settled with Oliver, who was ready to start a family. He knew what he wanted. I didn't. At least I didn't feel like I wanted the same things he did. In my diary, I wrote, "He has a ten-year plan already. I am just part of his plan. I want to develop a plan with someone. Together." I broke up with him a week before his board exam. He was devastated.

For a long while, we didn't speak to each other. Then I reached out and said hello eleven years after the breakup. I thought of him as a good friend now. With this big decision in my life, I asked for his opinion, still remembering and trusting his sound judgment.

He thought my desire to have my own children was only natural and strong, as it was for many women. There were several reasons having a child was desirable, but he wanted to play the devil's advocate regarding why *I*—not women in general—shouldn't have a child by myself. He didn't want me to be an SMBC.

Oliver pointed out that, although it was great to have children—and he loved his—he knew a number of very fine childless couples who were happy by themselves. Being an SMBC would complicate any future romantic relationships, and I had to be prepared to raise the child alone with its many financial, emotional, logistical, and physical demands. These responsibilities were not for the faint of heart. They could even cause a flare-up of schizophrenia. The consequences of parenting with that type of illness could have a profound impact on my child-rearing capabilities, and I would not be able to count on a husband if I were to become sick.

I told him it was possible I might become sick again, but that was a risk every parent took. If, unfortunately, I became incapable of taking care of my child or died in an accident, someone would have to step in. Of course, having a partner would provide a safety net, but I wouldn't have that right now, and that was okay. There were plenty of single mothers in this world who made it work. I would write up a will that would clearly state the person to whom I would hand my responsibilities. That was as much planning as I could do. I didn't think that because of my condition, I should have avoided being a mother completely. I told him I had talked to my psychiatrist and my regular doctor, and both were on board with my decision. I assured him that I'd definitely be careful and thoughtful as I headed down the path of single motherhood.

Then Oliver talked about a support network. Young people often move away from their parents as a sign of independence. But after having children, many people generally moved closer to and got help from their parents and relatives, which made life easier. This was true even for couples with children. He was concerned about the level of support I might need and not get on my journey. Although I'd have the support of my many friends in Boston, I couldn't underestimate the commitment a child required—a commitment that only I, not my friends, could provide.

He'd brought up difficult issues to consider since I didn't know exactly what I would need as a single mother. I told him that, for a few months, I'd been making as many mental checks on myself as possible. I'd heard from friends who had stories about challenging kids: some didn't sleep at night, some didn't eat, or they started to work late to avoid having to come home and face family problems. Parents were tired, and I could see for myself that they had to plan way ahead of time before meeting me for something as simple as dinner. There were good things and bad things about having grandparents around, traveling challenges, moving for kids to be in better school districts, and changing positions to get more flexible time, even if that meant losing a satisfying job. I took mental notes and asked myself, *Are you ready for this?* That was as much preparation as I could do at the moment. I couldn't predict the future, but I would do my best to plan for it.

At this point, I prepared myself to do everything on my own. Anything else I got help with would be extra. At some point in the process, I was introduced to a single, divorced mother who did not have much, but she figured things out one challenge at a time. I thought I was capable of doing that too. I didn't know what roles my parents might end up taking, but there were many people who didn't have direct support from their mothers or fathers. How I would raise my kid would not be the same as how my friend Oliver was raising his, with support and help from his parents.

I also had to consider what Oliver said when he took our conversation to a higher level. To him, life was about soul searching, finding out what made you happy, and embarking on that journey. At times, the end of a journey was what mattered, but other times, the journey itself was more important. I had friends who were married in their twenties and others who married in their thirties and beyond. To me, finding someone and getting married was about maturity, not age.

He also questioned my desire to have a child. "How do you know that this is not just a phase? Is having a child what you truly value?" I admitted to him that my desire was recent. He said in terms of what is healthiest, most women should ideally have their last pregnancy before the age of thirty-five. After that, there were more risks, and pregnancy complications such as high blood pressure, preeclampsia, and gestational diabetes increased. The rate of birth abnormalities or genetic conditions in babies also rose with the mother's age. Working backward, a woman should get married no later than her early thirties. Had I known I wanted children ten years ago, I could have focused my energy on finding a partner. If I hadn't known ten years ago, how could I know now that I'd still want children later? "Will this choice to be an SMBC still be a good decision in ten years?"

We knew we were not going to agree on this over long emails. He suggested I speak to my local support group for SMBC to help make a decision. I told him I was already speaking to single mothers in Boston and finding out what their journeys were like.

With regard to my age, I said my body would decide. The doctor I was seeing specialized in artificial insemination. I also had a great doctor at Mass General Hospital, which had world-class facilities and access to the rest of the health system network in Boston. There would be many professional people to help me through this process and run advanced tests if they saw a need. I thought, *Honestly, thirty-six is better than forty-six, right?*

On August 24, 2010, unlike most of my mornings, I woke up really early. I took my BBT and then peed in a cup for the ovulation tests. August was the third month I kept track of my cycles. Amazingly, the OPK turned, as the doctor said it would. All three of my OPKs—from CVS, ClearBlue, and First Response—showed positive for a luteinizing hormone surge, which is what triggers ovulation twenty-four to thirty-six hours later. I could not fall back to sleep. I sent an email to the office to say I would be taking a vacation day that day.

While I waited for time to pass, I was afraid I'd accidentally fall asleep and miss the time to call Dr. Smith's office. I set my alarm for 8:59 a.m. and lay in bed. Then I opened my iPad and read work emails. It was much better to do something, but I couldn't really focus on reading. I ended up checking emails and browsing Facebook. Good old Facebook for passing time.

At 8:58, I called the clinic. A woman picked up, and I recognized her voice. I told her who I was and that I wanted to come in that day. She said she'd call back after figuring out who was around to handle the procedure. *Okay . . . I'm okay waiting.* It was expected. This time, I started reading, and my mind didn't have trouble focusing on my book.

Thirty minutes later, no one had called back. I thought perhaps at this crucial moment, I'd given the woman the wrong phone number. I called again. She had not tried to call me back because it took her a while to find out when the doctor could meet with me. She called back in five minutes, apologized for making me wait, and asked if I could come right away. I said I could. I'd already taken a day off from work, which was good planning on my part. This was a priority!

With a whole summer of sunshine, of course it had to rain that day. But that didn't stop me. I took the T to Alewife and walked to the clinic in a downpour while looking forward to what came next.

The insemination was actually very much like a pap smear test. The vial holding my future was a very small clear glass jar, smaller than my thumb. Astonishing. I remembered the woman at the clinic confirming that my tank had arrived. *Tank? This little thing?* Then I was shocked that I was surprised. *Come on . . . think about it logically! How big of a container do sperms need?* The procedure didn't take long. I didn't feel anything at all, which startled me. I believed they knew what they were doing—they must have done this thousands of times. If there was anything unusual that occurred during the procedure, they would tell me.

Then I had to lie there. I thought positive thoughts for fifteen minutes. I thought of a little baby but didn't picture a specific gender because I knew I'd be happy with either. I thought of showing the world to the baby. I thought of the ocean. I thought of going to the beach. Taking a kid to school and summer camps.

When they came in to do the final check, both the nurse and the doctor asked if I was ready to be a mother, and I smiled and said, "Yes." It made me happy.

Rachel offered to drive me home from my appointment, but I said I was okay. During the next two days, I received texts from many girlfriends asking me how I was doing. Everyone was so excited for me.

I realized I'd had to decide for myself what kind of life I wanted to live. I could have talked to even more friends before going ahead with the procedure. Everyone had an opinion about my life, but I was the only one who would be responsible for a new life, a baby. No one could know what it was like to be a parent until they tried. I would do my best and figure it out as I went.

Two weeks later, I took a pregnancy test. It was negative. I was devastated and realized I'd had high hopes. I waited for my period, and it came right on time.

My mind went into overdrive. *Maybe this will take me years given my age. Maybe I will have to spend all my savings. Then I won't have any money left to take care of the baby.* Emotionally, I was not sure if I could take the disappointment month after month on my own. *Can I make the trip to the clinic each month and lie in that chair, hoping for a child to come?* I panicked. I imagined the worst outcome. I couldn't get myself to track my temperature anymore.

I thought about the one time I'd had sex without protection when I was in my early twenties. After that, I also couldn't sleep. I'd imagined the worst: *I will get pregnant.* The next day,

I could not focus at work at all. That night after work, I made my boyfriend take me to a clinic for a pregnancy test. I was so sure something was going to happen. I didn't know much about getting pregnant. It turned out I had nothing to worry about. My emotions were as high now as they'd been at that clinic. This was part of being a woman, being afraid to have babies during one part of life and wanting to have babies in another—the way only a woman could.

I remember feeling very much alone when I looked at the pregnancy test in my bathroom. I felt uncertain, weak, and hopeless, no longer brave. I didn't like the emotions I felt. The process required more willpower than what I had on my own. I needed to clear my mind and calm down. I picked myself up. I stopped focusing on getting pregnant. *I will take a break.*

A few months later, when Rachel gave birth to her second baby, I visited her at the hospital. When I held her newborn, who was just a couple of days old, I thought, *I'm glad I tried.* I'd felt the natural instinct of wanting to be a mother. Life would have been so different for me if I had succeeded, but it was not meant to be. I accepted that, believing I'd done what I could, but I couldn't control or predict everything in my life. I didn't regret not giving birth to a baby or not becoming a mother. With that acceptance and remembering how alone and sad I'd felt when my pregnancy test was negative, I was able to move on.

14

A SECOND CHANCE

I never thought of being a single mother by choice again. Instead, immediately after the failed IUI, I turned my full attention to schizophrenia, while my window of giving birth closed. I rechanneled my energy from trying to get pregnant into reliving my first schizophrenic experience. My mind sought something else to focus on. *I want to know what happened,* I said to myself repeatedly. *I want to find out the truth.* I was determined not to let the confusion about how I got this disease go on any longer. *I want a second chance, a do-over.*

When I thought about finding out the truth, I meant finding "Joe," redoing the behavioral mistakes I thought I'd made, and being a stronger person in the face of all things unfamiliar. Without medication, I went to look for my old schizophrenic experience, and schizophrenia answered back. I started hearing voices again. My friends got worried again. And then I had my second major schizophrenic episode while working at Medullan. It all started with me getting off my medication in order to have a baby. This time, it impacted my work. My mind no longer kept work and schizophrenia separate.

What do I want to do? I've been staying in the house all day for a few days. There must be a reason I keep going back to fragments of what I remember. It's like a CD skipping. Do you keep listening to the same CD, or do you get a new copy of the same CD? Or do you say, "Let me find a new CD"? The logical thing to do is to throw away the damaged CD. But it's stuck!

You are hearing voices. There are not that many important decisions in a person's life that one gets to make. You have to make them whether they are happy choices or not. Deciding that I am a schizophrenic, supposedly realizing once and for all that I am sick, does not seem to feel right. Talking to and hearing voices is what's here today. How many more days of this can I take? I don't know. But I do know that I can't live in two parallel worlds. I wonder how many people can keep secrets for the rest of their lives.

Laughing this minute and crying the next. Crying and laughing are typically very heartfelt things. It's healthy to do a lot of both. But if you are made to do it, it does not work.

In the middle of my confusion, I called Rachel. And in the middle of the call, my throat choked, and my voice broke as I was talking to her. I hung up quickly and was alone in my kitchen again. I thought about what was happening. Being alone allowed schizophrenia to dominate my mind completely. I didn't feel like it was me who was crying. So I got upset and spoke to the imaginary "folks in the room," who made my body cry: *Don't make me cry. I don't feel like crying.*

While alone, a few times I thought, *My body and my mind are separated.* I heard myself laughing before my mind had thought of laughing. *Can that be?* All of a sudden, work did not make any sense to me anymore. I was still going to the office, even though I knew something was wrong. "Freak out!"

I heard a voice say. I tried to close the company down once by telling everyone I was talking to in my mind to go home, wondering if I could confuse the people in the office with my thoughts. Not seeing any effect, I went to the café next door to see if there was anyone there who could read minds.

I knew something was very wrong, and I talked to Michael about my concerns. Everyone at work was very supportive and told me to take some time off for my health. It didn't seem right for me to go back to work until I solved my problem with the voices. I had to make a choice. *How do you want to live your life and spend your time? Do you want to think about your voices, or be productive and focused? While I'm at work, can I forget about all the craziness going on in my head at home?*

It's real. I have proof! Text. Email. Coffee shop. Around the same time that I heard a voice, I received a text from Michael. It was very early in the morning. *Why would he be up at this time?* I also got an email from the woman at HR. She told me to take some time off. *How does she know something's going on with me?* Then, in the coffee shop, I thought I saw someone turn to look at me, and at that same moment, I thought, *Look!*

Can you imagine having all your friends talking to you in your bedroom twenty-four hours a day, nonstop? I don't think this can happen, but I do believe that it is happening. And when I didn't hear it, I didn't remember it. My instincts told me my family and friends were "here" to help. It wasn't quite like having the radio or the TV on. Or was it? It wasn't all coming from one place. *I can't control the volume. I can't control the channel. And I can't turn it off. It comes on and goes whenever it wants. It stays as long as it wants.* When I answered my cell phone, I walked out of my bedroom to get privacy. But there was no one in my bedroom. I could recognize everyone's voice, just like hearing them on a phone call. *Except people from different stages of my life are converging.* I silently talked to everyone. Most of the time, people took turns. Sometimes we stuck to one conversation. Sometimes we jumped from topic to topic.

In the back of my mind, I tried to keep myself in check so that I wouldn't have another mental breakdown. *I can't believe this is really happening.* I thought about how hard it was to make this happen. *To organize this. To have everyone here. To care this much and stick with me until now!*

I think the hardest part of hearing voices was that they were there for me to listen to whether I wanted to or not. *This whole thing is wrong.* I kept checking with my gut about what was happening. *Gut check one: I failed. Gut check two: it's either failed, or I need to think more. What about gut check three?*

The first time I went through this at age thirty, I was happy; then it all went to hell. I didn't understand many of the things I experienced. I only missed a couple of days of work. The second time I was going through it six years later, there was a lot of crying. At first, I felt better, figuring things out—redoing the mistake I made the first time and correcting my confused thinking—and doing what I wanted to do. But then the voices showed up everywhere, even at work. I couldn't believe I fell asleep at work once and then another time in the subway on the way to see clients. I wanted to figure it out. I wanted to know what happened. I wanted to remember.

"No one knows the answer," a clear and kind voice said. The voice of Rachel.

"No one knows what to do," I thought in response.

"If you think you are in charge—" another voice said. Michael.

"*Who is in charge?*" I asked in silence. There was no answer. *I want to be in charge and turn off this talking.*

"I don't think so," a voice responded to my thoughts. Another friend's voice.

"You are in charge," the first voice said.

"*No one wants to be in charge,*" I thought reactively. A few seconds passed by.

"Life and death," a voice said. I listened without responding. *Yes, this feels like life and death.*

"Who is it?" another voice said.

Everyone (the voices) wants me to do something.

After I stopped showing up for work for a couple of days, Michael came to see me on a weekday to make sure that I was alright alone at home. "I don't know if I can help you. Take some time off if you need to," he said after he had sat with me, listened for a whole day, and asked a few questions.

A few weeks later, when I was sitting on my bed not knowing what I could do to turn off the voices, Rachel called an EMT, who came knocking on my door. "Do you need help?" Two male strangers stood at the threshold. Feeling helpless and very much cornered, I answered yes and followed them, not knowing where they were taking me or how they might help. When I walked out of my building, I went into an ambulance, which swallowed me up and felt huge. I ended up in the ER at Mass General Hospital (MGH). Rachel joined me there soon after. Knowing whatever help might be on the way, I broke down in front of her, crying uncontrollably in her arms in the tiny waiting room. She stayed with me until she was asked to leave.

A doctor evaluated my condition, though I was mostly unresponsive. I remember feeling so tired because I hadn't slept in I didn't know how many days, and I finally fell asleep on a sofa in his office. MGH decided to send me to McLean, a psychiatric hospital in Belmont, Massachusetts. I was hospitalized for the first and only time in my life.

At McLean, I received comprehensive care from a group of healthcare professionals for the first time, unlike what I'd experienced with Dr. Han. The first few days, I focused on solving my mystery, finding out who all these people in my head talking to me were and how they could do that. I thought I was in the safest place I could be. It would be hard for any stranger who talked to me in my head to reach me, and that made me feel comforted to focus on my thoughts.

I remember explaining to my doctor and care team that I didn't want to take any medication in case there was nothing wrong with my brain. I remained logical about this whole experience. After a morning session with my doctor, it had finally clicked for me. *The voices were created by my brain.* I retraced my steps. I rethought through everything I was confused about. I was now thinking about it all in a new way.

At McLean, every morning during the week, I met with my care team, which included an attending psychiatrist, a resident psychiatrist, a medical student, a nurse, a clinical case manager/social worker, and a mental health specialist. During the day, some of these caregivers were sprinkled among the patients. I was encouraged to participate in group sessions, which was one form of therapy. Around five o'clock, someone checked in with me again. With so many people around me all the time—caregivers, guards, and patients—I felt like I was back in a college dorm.

Once I gained full awareness of what I was dealing with, what I had—a brain disease—I cooperated and took medication, which immediately removed any auditory hallu-cinations. With the help of my doctors and care team, I finally fixed my confused thinking. I made friends with patients of all ages and with different conditions in my locked unit. At certain times during the day, we were allowed to take walks outside with a guide. I also went once with all these younger male patients in my unit to an indoor basketball court avail-able to us with supervision.

Rachel and my other girlfriends took turns visiting me, making sure someone showed up during visiting times every day. My dad came up from New Jersey both weekends I was there—one time with my mother and a second time with my stepmother. Michael and his wife brought their baby son to visit me. *If a baby can come here and play, then I am at a good place.*

After two weeks of inpatient care, I was discharged. My first psychosis was much more severe than this one, but this time, I got more help. More friends knew about what I was going through and tried to help me. Being admitted to McLean also finally made me truly comprehend the brain disease I had. My broken brain created my experience. Following my treatment at McLean, I spent the next few years learning about schizophrenia, reading as many books on the subject as I could find. To make myself useful, I also started participating in clinical research and began sharing my story publicly. I even wrote a book about it, *Becoming Whole: A Memoir.*

The irony is that once I was better, I was able to use my personal experience with schizophrenia on the job. Medullan worked exclusively with healthcare, and my department, technology, covered many areas. One day, my work became personal.

"I have a new project I thought you might be interested in," Michael said to me.

"What is it?"

"It's about schizophrenia." I stared at him, speechless. We created software solutions for many different conditions before, but this one was directly relevant to me. "Would you be interested in being part of that project?" The goal was to create an app that would help people like me.

"I would love to."

"Do you think you'd be open to sharing that with our clients? It might come up if you end up working on it."

"Of course I don't mind. I hope they'll be okay with it."

The project lead shared my condition with the client lead, and he was more than positive. "It would be great to have her."

Since my experience at McLean, combined with going back on medication at thirty-seven, I have not experienced any symptoms in the last decade except for one minor hiccup due to a stressful event at work. At the time, my psychiatrist increased the dosage of my medication, and everything quickly returned to normal again. That hiccup lasted less than a week. To this day, ten years after my stay at McLean, I am healthy and balanced when it comes to my mental and emotional health. My psychiatrist, therapist, friends, and family stay close and I have built a strong support network.

15

ROOTS

After trying to be a single mother and having been a patient at McLean, I'd been working for almost a year when I had a revelation: *I am going to do this!*

I immediately asked my boss for a one-on-one meeting. I sat in a black chair across from her in our office in Watertown, Massachusetts. She'd hired me the year before to manage her research group. We often met to talk about the goals and progress of my group of five researchers. Today, however, something different was on the agenda.

She finished up a call and smiled. "So, tell me, what do you want to talk about?"

I thought back to the moment when I'd had the epiphany. I'd been taking the bus home one evening, which usually took about an hour and a half. In the dark, as the bus drove through the empty, narrow streets, I saw my life flash before me, and the words that came to me when I thought I might have breast cancer returned: *I could die tomorrow.* It had been two years since I'd been hospitalized. I'd gained more awareness of schizophrenia. I'd just taken a two-week vacation in Taiwan and loved it. My old job hadn't felt fulfilling, so I'd changed jobs, but now the same feeling came to me with the current job. These jobs were both at great healthcare companies, but my heart was not in them. *Do I want to be doing what I'm doing right now? In five years? Ten years? Am I going to live the rest of my life just going between home and work?* Something else felt more important to me than working.

"I'm giving my two-week notice," I said quietly before continuing. "There's nothing wrong here. I like my work and my team. But I'm going back to Taiwan so that I can really reconnect with my birthplace." I'd been so happy being with my family and revisiting my homeland. At this time in my life, I could take full advantage of my freedom. I didn't have to consult with anyone about moving across the Pacific Ocean. I could afford the trip back and was able to survive on my savings for some time, living cheaply in Taiwan and staying with family. I was not worried about not having a job. I could always find another one. My parents were healthy and independent, so I didn't have to worry about them. I didn't have a detailed plan, but it felt right. Being single and independent, I could make this decision on my own for myself.

"I'm not surprised," she said. "You looked so happy when you came back from your trip. This makes sense. I'm happy for you."

"I want to spend more time with my grandmother and everyone else in Taiwan. Thank you so much for being so understanding."

Two weeks later, on my last day, my manager gave me a going-away package: a notebook with a cover picture of postal stamps, a plane, and luggage, plus a travel box to store souvenirs. "I hope you have a wonderful time traveling."

The following weekend, at the next dinner date with

Rachel, I explained, "My grandma is ninety-six. She's not going to wait forever for me to visit again. Seeing her for two weeks made me realize that I need to make this trip. I also want to reconnect with my birthplace. I wonder if I can find some old classmates from elementary school."

I felt a strong desire to get to know my roots. I had become a US citizen right after college and never looked back at Taiwan except for the occasional times when I reviewed some letters from my past. I had a box filled with handwritten Chinese letters sent to me from classmates and relatives in Taipei twenty-something years ago. I had sorted them by name. On the back of each envelope, I'd written down the date I'd received each letter. I'd gotten most of them by the time I turned fourteen, all within three years after moving from Taipei to New York City. After that, the letters slowed down and then stopped. I had stopped writing and reading Mandarin and speaking Taiwanese and Chinese. I didn't know anything about Taiwan anymore—its pop culture, news, food, or people. I reread a few of the letters and felt more certain about wanting to find out where I came from.

After quitting my job, I put my apartment up for sale. I managed the move like a work project. Productive every day, I worked toward leaving Boston. I told my friends that everything I owned was up for grabs and asked if anyone wanted my possessions. My sofa: picked up and gone. Dining set: gone. Bed and dresser: gone. I packed up bags and bags of books and donated them to the Boston Public Library. I had no hard feelings about parting with my furniture, but my books were hard to give up. In my apartment, my long hallway had been lined with shelves packed with biographies, memoirs, novels, how-to guides, cookbooks, travel books, and children's books.

I hit the limit of how many books I could donate to the library at once. Whatever else I had went to Goodwill. I discovered things I didn't even remember I had. I'd been holding on to clothing from college that no longer fit. It took a lot of effort to go through everything. I realized I'd packed a lot of material things into my 750-square-foot apartment, and I probably didn't need most of what I'd accumulated. It felt like peeling off layers of dead skin.

I told my doctors I was leaving Boston. Dr. F, my psychiatrist, wrote a letter to my future doctor in Taiwan for me. He also gave me a travel prescription for three months' worth of medication. I didn't know if I'd be able to find doctors as wonderful as Dr. F, Dr. Holbert (my primary care physician), or Dr. Beal (my dentist).

Because I didn't know how long I'd be separated from the possessions to be stored at my dad's home in New Jersey, I put together a compact photo album of all my US family and friends, of everyone important to me. I put that in my suitcase along with my medications. If I needed anything else, I could always buy it.

On my last Friday in Boston, Rachel and a few other girlfriends arranged for one last get-together before I left. We sat in a circle on the floor in my empty apartment. Everyone brought chips and drinks. We used paper plates and cups since I no longer owned any silverware. I couldn't contain my excitement in front of my girlfriends.

"Here. From all of us." Rachel held out a gift.

"Oh, you shouldn't have. You are all too nice!" I was not expecting any gifts but wasn't surprised that they were as thoughtful as always. I opened the red wrapping paper and saw a framed picture of all of us at Rachel's fiftieth birthday party at an elegant hotel in downtown Boston. I remembered that night. Everyone was there. The dancing. The singing. The laughing. I looked at the six of us in a row all dressed up and all smiles.

"We want you to remember us. You can see us no matter how far away you are."

"This is so perfect. Thank you. I'm going to miss you."

"What's your plan in Taipei?" Rachel asked.

"I am going to live with my aunt Christina. She has a spare room. My other aunt, uncle, and grandmother live in the same building downstairs. I'll figure out the rest when I get there. Anything is possible." I thought only of the future and not the past.

A light and cheerful mood filled the room. "You're so brave." "I wish I could pick up and move to another country." "This is it!" "Very exciting." "Hope you have a great adventure." "Don't forget us!" I said my goodbyes to my dear friends.

The next day, the last weekend at my apartment, my dad and stepmother drove from New Jersey to pick me up. To my horror, being frugal, they wanted to stay with me, sleeping on air mattresses in my messy living room. I didn't go along with that and booked a hotel room two blocks away. For two days, we cleaned my place and made some final trips to Goodwill. I kept a few boxes of things that were sentimental and important for me to keep. They helped me load the boxes into their two cars. On Sunday, my stepmother and I took a final look at my apartment: empty, clean, and ready for its next owner. I loved this place; it was the first apartment I'd owned. It brought me many great memories: wine parties and dinner dates with friends, quiet and alone time with myself. The location was great, right in Back Bay, with a small market around the corner, a Chinese restaurant and laundromat downstairs, three short blocks to the T stop, and across the street from the bus. The apartment had done so much for me. I closed my door for the last time and left Boston without looking back. Boston had been home for the last sixteen years. I was leaving the one place I'd known since becoming an adult.

All of a sudden, I felt lighter. On the way to New Jersey, I talked excitedly—the beginning of a new adventure. I wasn't tied down to a city anymore. I took advantage of this and spent a month with my dad and stepmother. It was symbolic to stop by Millburn, New Jersey, a place where I'd gone to high school before going to Cornell and then moving to Boston. I made the exact trip in reverse now. As an adult, I hadn't spent much time with my parents. Now we had dinner together every night. I felt very much loved. And with that wonderful feeling, I bought a one-way ticket to Taiwan. I got on the plane with just two suitcases.

The plane took off on time from Newark Airport. Cathay Pacific Airline didn't have a direct flight to Taipei and had a layover in Hong Kong. Taiwan is located south of Japan and Korea, east of China, and north of the Philippines—about the size of Maryland with about twenty-three million people. My full flight teemed with mostly Asian people, and I heard familiar sounds of Taiwanese, Chinese, and Cantonese. To stay calm, I decided to sleep through the trip like I had done before when flying to Taipei. My ability to do that during a long flight—about fourteen hours—was one of my superpowers. When I awoke, I made a mental list of all the things I needed to do right away: Get a phone. Find a doctor. Look for my old classmates.

I landed in Hong Kong, where I finally had a moment and

pinched myself. *I quit and sold my place in two months. This is really happening. I'm almost there.* I let that sink in a bit. Even though the last leg only took an hour and forty minutes, it felt so much longer.

My cousin Calvin, three years younger than me, came to pick me up at the airport. As I walked out of the customs area through the double doors, having no trouble reading signs in Chinese, I searched for him. Among all the people with black hair, I spotted him waving and smiling at me. "Mindy, here! Here!"

Calvin looked older and heavier. We hugged and laughed. "Hey, sis, good to see you again. Is this all you have? I was worried about fitting everything in my car. You didn't bring ten pairs of shoes?" Then he handed me an old smartphone. "This is for you. I have a spare."

Every time we were together, I envisioned the young version of him in my mind. For me, he would always be my little Calvin hanging on to my shirt, following me everywhere I went. Calvin laughed and said, "Do you remember when you were going downtown to roller skate? You didn't want me to tag along, but I did anyway. Remember I wanted to go with you everywhere you went?" I remembered the indoor roller skating rink and Calvin skating behind me. We'd circled the rink as fast as we could. That was so much fun. I was now back in the place where people knew me as a little kid.

Before going to my aunt's, Calvin took me straight to a night market for a snack: Taiwanese crispy, salty chicken. He knew I loved that and always got it when I visited. We talked nonstop, trying to catch up as much as we could squeeze in. I spoke in middle-school-level Chinese even though I never spoke it in Boston, while he mixed in Chinese and English in case it was easier for me. He was busy with work. My uncle and aunt—his parents—were doing well. He played the latest popular songs for me in the car. He would take me to many more night markets after that first night.

My aunts Theresa and Christina welcomed me with open arms. Both had small frames and were slightly shorter than me. They had always been close and had similar haircuts and clothing. Instead of the long, straight black hair I remembered as a kid, they both kept their hair short, right above the shoulder, with some gray streaks in it. Ever since I was little, my aunts were always elegantly dressed in fitted black cashmere sweaters and gray cotton pants. Aunt Theresa no longer taught piano, whereas Aunt Christina continued her work at a large retail clothing company.

Aunt Christina had prepared the spare room she'd told me about. Luckily for me, my aunts lived in the same building, both three-bedroom apartments, in a great area called Qingtian Street near Daan Park, with plenty of nearby public transportation. I wouldn't have to drive and could manage on foot as I did in Boston.

Decades ago, before moving to America, as I mentioned before, I'd grown up with Grandpa, Grandma, Aunt Theresa, Aunt Christina, Calvin, his parents, my younger cousins Jimmy and Michelle, and their parents. Even though in the last twenty or so years, I'd only visited Taipei a couple of times, every time I saw them, I felt completely at home.

When I arrived at Aunt Theresa's, everyone was still up, although it was almost midnight. I was excited to see her, Uncle Sam, Aunt Christina, and Grandma and hugged them. To that, my grandma responded, "Here is an American child.

That's why she does this hug thing." I was there in January for two weeks. Five months later, I'd moved here.

Grandma—petite, about my shoulder height, and sporting shining gray hair—looked conservative in a light-gray knee-length skirt and a yellow shirt with white daisies. Still alert at age ninety-six, she kept track of what everyone did at home. She sat at her usual spot on the right of the sofa with Aunt Christina to her left. Uncle Sam and Aunt Theresa perched on the loveseat. Over the years, Aunt Theresa had collected a house full of things tightly packed into all the open spaces against the walls.

The first married couple I was truly aware of was my grandparents since my mother had been away in New York studying for her PhD when I was a little girl. I lived with my father and grandparents and saw the love between the two of them and for their children and grandchildren. Grandpa handled everything outside of the house, and Grandma managed everything inside. Every day, without change, Grandpa bought groceries from the local market, and Grandma cooked all of our meals. My grandmother also washed our laundry and cleaned. In the afternoons, they took naps together. They worked together to provide a loving home for us. Their love was quiet, peaceful, and steady.

Grandma was very much a traditional woman. The fact that she'd been living for ninety-six years was amazing to me. Just imagine what she'd seen in her lifetime—before telephones, radios, and televisions, before cars and planes, before both world wars. I loved talking to my grandmother. Her life was the exact opposite of my single life. Grandma married young to my handsome and tall grandfather, who'd been educated at a Japanese school. They owned and ran a grocery store together and sold wholesale to the rest of the island. When they were young, business was good for a while. After being married, Grandma gave birth to eight children. Her life centered around her husband and kids, and she seldom left the house. As a young woman, she was a talented tailor, but she never pursued a career in fashion. She stayed home helping my grandfather with his business and taking care of her children. When Grandpa's business ran into trouble, he closed down the store. They both retired and did whatever they could for their grown children. When my mother left Dad and me for school in the United States, my grandparents moved in with us. That was how I came to live with them as a kid growing up.

From the age of seven to fourteen, I had my grandparents and father for my role models. My dad's two younger brothers were also married. Calvin's parents and the parents of my youngest cousins, Jimmy and Michelle, also influenced my childhood. Calvin's parents tended to challenge each other. Jimmy and Michelle's were kinder. Like any other child, I soaked in everything from my big family. My core as a person was seeded and heavily influenced by them all.

Soon after I turned fourteen, my dad and I moved to New York City to join my mother when she was sick. Dad told me, as he believed at that time, "This is just a temporary move. We'll go home soon." Both my father and I came on visas declaring us dependents of my mother, who was in the United States on a student visa.

I didn't speak any English but knew the alphabet from the first year of middle school. In Taiwan, middle-school students took English as a second language (ESL), but I hadn't learned much. To make sure that I integrated fully into my environment, my mother decided to enroll me in a local middle school near Columbia University. The school had predominantly Hispanic and African American students. The teachers there decided I should attend the gifted class and not the ESL class so that I would learn English and not Spanish. Four girls in the gifted class took me under their wing and helped me order lunch. I had bagels and pizzas and cold-cut sandwiches for the first time in my life. I loved egg bagels with cream cheese and pepperoni pizza with extra cheese but had a hard time ordering sandwiches on my own. I didn't know any of the meats, cheeses, or sauces. I started speaking English after a month of being mute. I excelled at mathematics and science because I had already studied some of those materials in Taipei. Being the first Asian student in the school, I was asked by a boy in my class if I knew kung fu during recess in the courtyard. I showed him what I knew from my gym class in Taipei. He was impressed. I felt welcomed by both teachers and students and settled right into New York City.

"Was it hard to move from Taipei to New York?" Michael once asked me.

"As a kid, I adjusted quickly. I'm glad I moved here when I was young." The hardest part was leaving my family and friends in Taipei. But after a while, I stopped missing them and made new friends. I aimed to assimilate and be as American as I could. Right before applying for college, my parents and I received our green cards. We could live here permanently. I had since forgotten Dad's promise that this move to America was temporary. Fortunately, thanks to my green card, I could also apply for financial aid for college.

At eighteen, I got into Cornell and wrote a letter to my grandfather telling him all about that. He sent back a long letter saying how proud he was that his granddaughter was going to the same college as the Taiwanese president. My grandfather passed away due to an asthma attack shortly after he wrote me that letter. I didn't quite process his passing until many years later. To me, I pictured him writing Chinese calligraphy in his study or holding my little hand to go grocery shopping in the nearby market. My grandma would go on living without him, by this time, at least twenty years.

At this point in time, Grandma's focus in life became Aunt Theresa, Uncle Sam, and Aunt Christina. The rest of her children had either moved out of the city or migrated from Taiwan. She lived a very peaceful life, mostly spending her time with family—exactly what she wanted.

After moving to New York and finishing high school—before I went to Cornell—I used all of my babysitting and tutoring money to buy plane tickets to Taiwan. As an eighteen-year-old, I had been so excited to go back and see everyone. But when I arrived in Taiwan, I was shocked at how everything looked so unfamiliar. My grandpa had passed away, and both my old home and the city of Taipei had changed.

During that trip, I made plans one night to go out with my elementary-school classmates. As I got ready to leave, my grandma got mad at me. "Are you here to see and spend time with your family? Why are you going out by yourself? It's dangerous." I was told I couldn't go out alone because I was a "kid." "Your father has trusted me to take care of you. We are responsible for you." I looked at her, speechless. In Millburn as a teenager, I was independent and free to go anywhere I wanted. Dad and Mother never stopped me. Out of respect, I couldn't argue with my grandma, but I cried in front of her since she didn't want me to leave the house. This was not how I imagined my first trip back to Taipei would be.

Everyone else in the family heard about this "fight." Calvin offered to be my chaperone. He was a boy who had grown up in Taipei, and even though he was three years my junior, my family accepted that he could take care of me outside of the home because he was male and knew the ropes. That's just how it was perceived back then. To make my life easier, my uncles and aunts suggested I sleep over with them some nights.

I didn't realize this at the time, but I do now: America had changed me, and my grandparents hadn't changed with me. And I was too young at eighteen to reconcile the two cultures. A week later, I ended my first trip back to Taiwan and didn't think about visiting again for a long time.

When I visited this time, after I walked in and hugged Grandma, she gave me a set of keys to the house. Seeing her after being away for so long, I was keenly aware of how much she had aged. Petite with a small frame, she had a very gentle and kind personality. She didn't say much, but when she did, it was always direct and to the point. She had a full head of beautiful silver hair. She'd cut it short, so it was easier to manage. She came up to my shoulder, and I was five-foot-six. She wore skirts, never pants. She always sat upright on the sofa and didn't know how to lean back and be lazy. She didn't remember any Japanese from her childhood—she'd been adopted by Japanese parents. The tradition when someone had a miscarriage was to adopt a young child to compensate for that sad incident. She didn't cook or clean anymore. Even though she moved slowly, she was still healthy and mobile.

She still could do math in her head, which led to my aunts saying that she had a "gold brain."

One day during my stay, I decided to cook dinner. I remembered my favorite dish as a kid was the hot lunchbox that Grandma had prepared for me every day when I was in elementary school. I asked her, "Would you please tell me how to make soy sauce stew with pork and egg?"

"Oh, I don't remember how to make it anymore." She laughed. Nowadays, Aunts Christina and Theresa cooked. They didn't like Grandma to use the stove, thinking that was dangerous.

"Really? But I love that dish."

"Okay. Let's see." She told me what ingredients to get from the supermarket. After I came home, I went straight to the kitchen, while she sat in the living room in her usual spot. From there, she instructed me on what to do.

"Wash the pork with hot water? Really? Got it." I never thought that pork was dirty before, but the clean water became muddy and a little bloody. "The eggs are boiled, and I took off the shells. Soy sauce . . . this much?" I showed Grandma the spot. "More? More?" Then it was the same with rice wine. "More? I should put more?" I also threw in lots of garlic.

"Grandma, it's all done. I guess now we wait." She didn't tell me how many hours I should leave it on the stove, but I assumed three or four, which would just be in time for dinner when everyone came home from work.

"Wow. You cooked," Aunt Theresa said proudly as all of us sat around a round table in the dining room. It was a tradition to eat dinner together with Grandma. Aunt Theresa always made sure that whatever we had for dinner was edible for Grandma. I was told she could only eat food that was soft and cut into small bite-sized pieces. She also couldn't eat anything that was too salty or had too much sauce.

"Yeah, Grandma helped me," I said.

"Tastes good. This is good. Very good," Grandma said as she took the first bite. Cooking for one versus cooking for my family was different. Watching Grandma eat what I'd made gave me great satisfaction.

I felt like a ten-year-old again, warm and loved. I'd found what I'd come looking for: the extended family—Grandma, uncles, aunts, and cousins I'd known before I moved to America—all still here. Even after years of separation, I had recognized their mannerisms and way of living immediately. They were familiar but at the same time aged. They still loved me just as I remembered. Grandma represented everything I knew about Taiwan.

It occurred to me that my life as an older woman would be very different from Grandma's. I didn't have children, so I wouldn't live my older days like her. If I make it to ninety, I picture myself living in an assisted home. I would need just one room. I'd be comfortable in a cozy, small space because I'll probably not move about too much with my weak knees. In the room, I'd have my essentials: photos of my parents, relatives, friends, and even my friends' kids. I'd have plants because I like having something alive in my living space. I'd have a few of my favorite books, though my eyesight would probably not be too good. The room would be in a building filled with elders like me—a retirement community with a nurse on staff to keep us healthy and a doorman to keep us safe. Hopefully, there would be a chef on staff as well so I could eat a couple of small meals each day. I'd spend my days reading and writing. Sometimes my friends' grown kids might visit me. I'd have nice neighbors in the building. I'd be alone but not lonely. If I was lucky, I'd be free of major diseases and still have a sharp mind and live my old age in peace. When I gave out my last breath, someone would be there to take care of my business. I would be okay with this.

Three years after my trip home, my grandma passed surrounded by my aunts, uncles, and cousins. I am more than grateful I'd had this opportunity to be with her again.

Not everyone I grew up with was still in Taipei. Two of my dad's younger brothers and their families had moved away. During my thirties, I felt this gap in my life, which came from losing touch with my uncles, aunts, and cousins who were now spread over Los Angeles, Vancouver, and Taipei. An only child, I grew up with my paternal grandparents, Dad, three of his younger brothers, their wives, two of his younger sisters, and one of their husbands. When I moved to New York, three younger cousins and many more second cousins lived nearby. I had wonderful memories of my childhood.

Los Angeles and Vancouver didn't seem that far from Boston. I decided to visit them after not having seen them for twelve years, which was fifteen years before I made the big journey back to Taiwan again. Shortly after breaking up with Chris, I visited Vancouver first. I knew very little about the current lives of my uncle, aunt, and two cousins, even though I'd grown up with them. They had owned a tea shop in Taipei. I always remembered how their apartment smelled: earthy, minty, floral, and spicy. I didn't know what would happen when I saw them again, but I knew they were important to me.

My cousin Jimmy picked me up at the Vancouver International Airport. He'd grown up enough to drive a car by then. At first, he didn't recognize me, and I hadn't spotted him either. I called him on his cellphone, and it turned out that he was standing right behind me. He said my name energetically and smiled at me. No longer a skinny little boy, he was a full-grown and built man, the same height as me, with an almost fully shaved haircut. I gave him a hug, which he awkwardly accepted.

Uncle Frasier and Aunt Tina waited right by their front door to greet me. They hadn't changed a bit and looked just as I remembered—their faces, their voices, their caring. Childhood memories from Taiwan rushed through my mind: going to the park with Jimmy when he almost broke his nose falling from a monkey bar under my supervision, Jimmy locking Grandma outside in the backyard while the stove was on, Jimmy flushing a towel down the toilet, holding little Michelle when she was still a baby. We talked and tried to catch up as much as possible. I was glad that my Mandarin and Taiwanese held up. I told them how I was doing, and they told me how they were. Finally, after three hours, it had gotten so late that we all reluctantly said goodnight.

My uncle and aunt took me to all the cool spots they knew in the area: Queen Elizabeth Park, Granville Island, Gastown, and Chinatown—just as they did in Taipei. I felt immediate comfort. A lot had happened in twelve years. They had moved because they wanted to give my cousins a better future. Uncle had come over first with both of his children, who were in middle and elementary schools at the time. Aunt sold their home and followed eight months later. Now my cousin Jimmy was a chef and cooked at a Chinese restaurant. Michelle was finishing college.

Knowing how frugal they must have been, I was surprised when they took me to the Top of Vancouver Revolving

Restaurant for dinner. The incredible view served as a great backdrop to the precious time we spent together.

Our family gatherings had always involved endless eating. That was how we enjoyed life. It was no different in Vancouver. One night, instead of going out, we had a hot pot for dinner. Aunt Tina made her own version, which used a special soup. In an electric pot, the soup came to a simmer. On the table, there were raw ingredients such as thinly sliced beef, pork, and lamb; baby bok choy; Napa cabbage; tofu; and baby corn. Everyone picked their favorites and cooked them in the hot soup. To cool the hot food a bit, we dipped it in a bowl of raw eggs mixed with Bullhead barbecue sauce. Drinking the soup at the end of the meal was the best. The soup had the great flavor of the essence of everything that we had cooked in it. I hadn't had hot pot in a while—it was delicious, familiar, and sentimental.

After a week, my cousin Jimmy and my aunt took me to the airport. Amazed at how fast the time went by, I regretted having such a short trip. How wonderful to visit them and get caught up once again. They seemed different but familiar at the same time. My "little" cousins were all grown up and able to live and stay close to their parents. I was happy to see they were all together and doing well. I promised myself not to wait another twelve years to see them again.

Shortly after Vancouver, I went to Los Angeles to see my other uncle. My dad's youngest brother, Uncle Mike, had gotten married after Dad and I left Taipei. I'd never met his wife, Sue, nor my cousins Julie and Jane.

Seeing my uncle at the airport, I felt so emotional. I remembered one time when we were both still in Taipei, he had gone to Japan and brought home a table of small souvenirs and toy figures: a few cars and planes and small statues of people dressed in traditional clothing. He told me, "You can pick one for yourself. Any one!" He was always generous with us kids. He was still as good-humored as I remembered him to be. "Eat as much as you can while you are here. Nobody will watch you. Get big. You can go on a diet when you go home." I met my new aunt Sue and cousins Julie and Jane, and they welcomed me with kindness. We didn't talk much at the beginning because we didn't share a past, but Uncle Mike made sure I had a good time. He took me to Disney, Hollywood, Rodeo Drive, and his favorite weekend hangout: the Mexican flea market. The conversation poured. I got to know Aunt Sue better while she and I took daily walks to Redondo Beach. Aunt Sue cooked Taiwanese dishes almost every meal except when Jane made a reservation at a Korean BBQ restaurant. Jane also got special snacks like beef jerky from Taiwanese stores, while Julie and I shared Taiwanese dessert shaved ice with mango.

At this time, I was the only person who had reconnected with all of Dad's brothers and sisters and their children again. To my uncles and aunt, I would always be the little girl they held in their arms in Taipei—the first baby in my generation. Since these trips, I've made a conscious effort to stay in touch with both families. I attended both of my cousins' weddings in Vancouver. When both families downsized, I visited them again. A few years later, Dad and his brothers and their wives also met up in Las Vegas for a week. I had found another important thing I had lost: family.

After these trips to Vancouver and Los Angeles, I also reflected on my relationship with my parents. I loved my dad but hardly saw or talked to him. He, my mother, and I lived our lives very independently. My cousin Chao, the son of my dad's cousin who studied at MIT, lived with me in 2011 after my hospitalization. Chao, tall, fit, articulate, and thoughtful, was four years younger than I was. He liked to keep his hair shoulder length and had many friends from school. During the Thanksgiving holiday, he suggested the two of us spend it in Millburn, New Jersey, to join my dad, my stepmother, and my stepbrother.

Before dinner, my cousin took a photo of us standing together in the dining room with the festive dinner on full display. "Let's remember this wonderful moment," he said. Chao took pictures of everything. He liked to document his life. I didn't remember the last time we had a family photo, but thanks to Chao, this became our family tradition.

Around the same time, my mother also asked me to reserve Christmas for her in Queens, New York. I now spend Thanksgiving with Dad and Christmas with Mother every year. We created something more than what we'd had.

I learned that family would always be there for me. It was never too late to find someone from the past or start a new family tradition.

Besides family, I also looked for my elementary-school classmates in Taipei. While I was still in Boston, I searched for the phone number of a classmate named Coco from some twenty years before. I told my cousin Chao about her, and he said he would track her down and make the call for me. Amazingly enough, when he called, Coco's father answered the phone, and he still remembered me—"the little girl who went to America." He gave my cousin Coco's new phone number. I was so excited to get in touch with her. When I got to Taipei, I contacted her at once.

Coco and I used to sit together in elementary school. Since we lived in the same neighborhood, I visited her home many times. When I made my first trip back to Taipei as an adult, Coco organized an outing for me with a few other old classmates. We rode motorcycles through the countryside near Taipei. She was the person who helped me get reconnected with everyone. We caught up by going out to eat. She remained slim and youthful with an elegant style. She was married, had a son, and kept in touch with a few others we both knew. Through her, I connected with more of my old classmates, including Jeff. I still had the letters we wrote to each other when I first moved to New York City. I had made copies of everything I wrote before mailing them. The letters were ordered according to people and dates.

Out of everyone I met up with again in Taipei, Jeff and I had the most to talk about. Like Coco, he and I used to be in the same class in elementary school, and he, too, kept in touch with Coco. Jeff and I wrote the most letters to each other during my first couple of years in New York. He asked me what the United States was like. I wanted to know about what he was doing with his free time. He also worried about the required military service, while I started to forget how to write some Chinese characters. He called me as soon as we found each other again. "It's you! Oh my goodness, how long has it been?" He was as excited about getting back in touch as I was.

Jeff owned an eyeglass store in downtown Taipei, where his wife worked with him. They had a son and a daughter. I asked him if I had changed, and he said, "You were much louder, more carefree, and energetic the last time I saw you." I had been fourteen years old at the time, so of course I acted more boisterous back then. He also said, "You were friendly to boys too, not just girls. You didn't mind us." It was unusual at the time because, back then, all the other girls kept to themselves.

I didn't remember much about the Taipei of my childhood. I went back to where I used to live, my old home. It still had metal panels, yet it was no longer blue but silver. Only the metal door looked familiar. The rest of the block was unrecognizable. I also went back to my elementary school, which looked so small and worn. As a child, I'd been free to roam to school, nearby parks, and shops within two to three blocks of home. The comic book store was no longer there. Those were my landmarks.

Now, I set to explore Taipei as an adult. At first glance, cars, scooters, and people packed the streets. At the markets, fruits could be found at all times. Taiwan was called the "king of fruit." There were eateries everywhere. For food, there were fancy restaurants and tiny holes in the wall. There were schools every three to four blocks. What I loved the most were the cafés. Because we lived in a district filled with schools, there were streets that had three to four cafés on a block. I made an effort to try a new one every week.

My cousin Chao was working on a new startup called Innovation Open House (IOH), which helped high-school students learn about colleges in Taiwan. Since I was in Taipei for an indefinite time, I thought I'd like to work on a good cause while I was there. He asked me to join him and be part of his company as the chief operating officer (COO). In Boston, I had thought about starting something of my own as well but never became serious about it. Now it seemed like a good time to be an entrepreneur. Through IOH, I met many talented, young college students and recent graduates who volunteered to work with us. Unfortunately, after a year, I realized I wasn't interested in education and left his startup. I wanted to focus on writing.

I asked one of my uncles, Chao's father, a journalist and editor, about writing. He asked why I wanted to write. "That's simple," I said. "Because I want to tell a different story about schizophrenia and how love and friendship can triumph over a broken brain."

His reaction was "Sounds like you have something to say. Well, then you have to say it." He understood that I needed to focus on writing and have no distractions. I didn't think I could write and work at the same time. I felt I didn't have much time, and writing took effort. I wanted to be good. I wanted to have depth.

One night, lying in bed, I thought about what I wanted to do with my life. I'd given myself until the end of the year to be income-free. I had ten months to follow my dream. I would support myself using my savings until then. I gave myself permission. *How will I use this time? What's the most important thing I want to do right now?* The more I thought about it, the more I wanted to leave IOH. *Can I write? I don't know. Am I special? Probably not.* My writing is not that literary, and I make grammar mistakes all the time. The only reason I would write full time is that I wanted to. I didn't expect I would get anything back. *I might die tomorrow!* I made the decision not to work at a regular job. I started spending my afternoons in cafés and wrote.

Life in Taipei quickly became settled. In the beginning, my trip focused on revisiting my past, but life was not just about what had happened in my childhood and youth. As I learned more from the past, I also started creating new life experiences with new friends.

Daisy, a friend of Chao's, came up with a suggestion one day. "I know this great yoga teacher. Want to try it? I can bring you to the studio for a free class."

Yoga interested me. I'd tried it once at a studio in Boston but had a hard time keeping up with everyone. I didn't understand any of the commands, and somehow I twisted my back, which hurt for a while. Since then, I hadn't tried it again. "I'm not sure yoga is for me." I explained to Daisy what I'd experienced.

"Sounds like you didn't pick the right class. This teacher I know is really good. Why don't you give it another try?" With a friend by my side, I felt brave and excited enough to give it a go.

The next day, Daisy took me to her yoga studio. Having her with me made it better, and she was right: this teacher had great patience. He both demonstrated and called out the poses. He also readjusted my pose when I sensed I was not doing it quite right, and I could follow his instructions. It felt challenging but not impossible. An hour and fifteen minutes flew by. After one class, I was hooked and did yoga every morning.

After my morning yoga class, I found different cafés to visit. There was a particular one near the studio that I both liked and found convenient. It had both bar and table seats. Since I was on my own, I usually sat at the bar. The decor was modern with mostly black and brown furniture, glass tabletops, and colorful pillows. It was usually half-packed with other coffee drinkers. The menu displayed coffee from different regions of the world. I learned about the nuances between cold brew and drip coffee. I didn't drink black coffee and ordered mostly lattes. They also had a few simple food dishes. My favorite lunch was salmon salad, light and delicious. After a while, I made friends with the baristas. It was very pleasant to be there following my yoga workout.

Every afternoon, I wrote about my experience with schizophrenia, which eventually became my first book. Finally, I had the time and mental space to write regularly. For six months, this was how I lived my single life: yoga, writing, and time with friends and family. My mind cleared and became uncluttered. My shoulders relaxed. I felt incredible.

My best friend from high school, Rose, still resided in Taiwan when I came to live there. She'd lived in Taiwan as a child as well. We'd actually met in New Jersey and hoped to go to the same college. Even though that didn't work out, we kept in touch. Now we were together again. One day during our coffee date, one of us mentioned Japan.

"That's another place I always wanted to visit," I said. "Remember all the comic books we used to read from Japan?"

Rose had studied Japanese in Japan for a year after college. She knew her way around Osaka and had no problem exploring Japan on her own.

"Really? We should go."

Rose asked me what kind of trip I wanted to have: historical and cultural or shopping. I told her definitely the former. A few weeks later, we were on our way to Kyoto and Osaka.

My grandparents had lived through the Japanese occupation in Taiwan and had grown up with Japanese culture and beliefs. When I was a little kid, I remembered my family watching Japanese TV and soap operas. Some of the food we loved to eat was influenced by Japanese cooking as well. There were also Japanese phrases mixed into our Taiwanese. During the four days that Rose and I were in Japan, everything felt just a little bit familiar and friendly.

My first impression of Japan was how clean and organized it appeared. At the airport, train station, and crossroads, people strictly walked on the right side. Rose knew these cities well and planned the whole trip. At our first meal, I was excited to sit on tatami mats while overlooking a beautiful garden in the center of the restaurant. Rose introduced me to *omurice*, the Japanese rice omelet flavored with ketchup. In Kyoto, we walked from temple to garden to temple. We drank the holy water at Kiyomizudera Temple to purify our bodies. At one of the smaller temples for love, Rose made me ring the bell and clap for good luck. Women wore beautiful kimonos. Rose explained that some of them were tourists renting traditional clothing for fun. We could identify the locals by how comfortably they walked in their kimonos. The Nishiki Market had all kinds of seafood, dry food, drinks, and candies. Rose and I shared a few fish dishes there, which reminded me of how Grandma used to cook fish at home when I was a little girl.

After a full day in Kyoto, Rose took me to a hot springs resort, which was one of my requests. The hotel room was traditional: an empty tatami room with a small square table in the center. After we checked in, Rose led us through the streets that wove through this small mountain town. For lunch, I had a simple *udon* entrée —white, round, and slightly chewy. A perfect texture and taste. The tiny restaurant had only six seats and was packed.

After an exploratory walk, we returned to the hotel. The whole focus for this day was the hot springs. Rose showed me how to enjoy them. Men and women were separated. First, we cleaned ourselves in the shower room. Then we went into a pool with hot water. I felt my muscles relax, and my whole body warmed. After about ten minutes, I got too hot, which was the perfect time to enter the cold pool, which felt amazingly comfortable. For several hours, I rotated between sitting in the hot or cold pool. There were also other kinds of pools: salty or muddy.

At one point, Rose asked, "Do you want to check out the outside?" There, we discovered a larger but shallower hot-spring pool with a gorgeous view of the mountains. We stayed outside for the rest of the afternoon.

For dinner, we were served about fifteen small bowls and plates for each person, which were all set on the table in the middle of our room. Again, there were lots of fish, eggs, and marinated and fermented vegetables. After dinner, the hotel server came to clean the table, put it away, and set up blankets on the tatami mats for us to sleep on. I had seen this kind of setup on TV shows when I was little.

"This was the perfect traditional trip," I told Rose. Traveling to Japan was an important item to check off my bucket list.

For seventeen months, I lived a very healthy lifestyle. I ate well, exercised daily, worked on what I loved, and had no major stress in my life. It was probably no coincidence that during this time, I was on the lowest dosage possible of schizophrenia medications without any symptoms or problems. I also lost weight without any conscious effort. Life felt very simple and good.

I felt connected to my birthplace and from there found my center. I had updated memories of my extended families and old classmates, people who were dear to my heart, as well as new friends. I knew Taipei again, this time as an adult: its streets, night markets, public transportation, shops, cafés, and restaurants. Its beauty and groundedness.

From where I lived at my aunt's place, there were at least

ten buses going in different directions along with a nearby subway station with modern and fast trains. The subway charged by distance and started at about one US dollar.

Our favorite restaurants, which were also Grandma's, were Shin Yeh Taiwanese Cuisine and Yuan Japanese Cuisine in Taipei. Shin Yeh had simple and authentic Taiwanese cooking that I recognized from home, such as preserved radish omelet, stir-fried pork liver, three-cup chicken, and sweet potato congee. At Yuan, we liked sashimi, pan-fried fish, grilled chicken, and beef. Enjoying meals with my family was priceless.

Being used to chain cafés like Starbucks and Caffé Nero, I was pleasantly surprised by the local cafés in Taipei. Each had its unique character. Most of the time, I would meet the young owners behind the coffee maker. On weekends, I dragged my aunts to try different cafés nearby. Each owner sourced their own coffee beans. Various desserts or salads were available at some. One had cats roaming freely among the guests. Another had a piano in the middle of the place, where patrons entertained each other with local and American music. Some were decorated with modern paintings. One reminded me of a Cape Cod vacation home with blue and white decor, seashells, and starfish. Most were small and cozy.

One day during my stay, after being there for seventeen months, we heard awful news. Without any warning, my youngest cousin, Julie, in California, whom I'd just gotten reacquainted with, fell sick, had massive bleeding in her brain, and passed away—all in one week. No one knew the cause or what she had. The whole family was in shock. She had been young and healthy. I wanted to help, so I bought a one-way ticket back to America and flew in a hurry to California from

Taipei. I couldn't imagine what Uncle Mike and Aunt Sue were going through, and I wanted to be there for them. Calvin felt the same and left Taipei with me. I didn't even get a chance to say goodbye to Grandma. We didn't let her know about our cousin.

In California, the family spent every day telling stories about Julie. A happy and outgoing young woman, she had just started working in sales for a car rental place. I created a video showing photos of her life. Her parents often cried together in silence. We took long walks. To fill some of this big gap in their lives, my uncle and aunt took care of Calvin and me for the two months we stayed there. Dad, as well as Uncle Mike's brothers and sisters, called often. There is nothing like the sudden death of someone young to make everyone treasure what they have. It hit home for me how much no one can predict what will happen in life. All I could do was live each of my days to the fullest. *Yes, any one of us could die tomorrow.*

After spending a couple of months with my uncle and aunt, helping them grieve and get back to a normal life, it was time for me to move on and get back to my own life. At this point, I felt it was time to go back to New England and not Taipei. I didn't have a concrete plan yet, but this time I'd left Taipei on my own terms and wasn't being moved by my mother. Even though I'd found my center and had reconnected with my family and culture, I felt strongly about identifying more as an American than anything else.

America was my other center and home. Much of my value and belief systems were rooted in American ideals. I had high regard for individualism, gender equality, political democracy, and liberty. In some ways, life in Taiwan felt like how I might like to live when I retired, writing consistently and regularly.

But I was too young to continue to live this way right now. I didn't want to live at my aunt's forever, and I didn't want to continue to live off my savings because I might end up having nothing later. It was time to be productive and make a living again. I wanted to live a rich and social single life rather than just a peaceful one.

I decided to stop by my dad's first and see what I could figure out regarding my next step. While I was in New Jersey, my friends in Boston invited me to visit.

"What are you doing alone in New Jersey? We miss you. Come and see us," Michael said. I brought a small suitcase and came back to Boston. For two months, I lived at my friends' homes: Rachel, Michael, Samantha, Paige, Vara, Zoe, and others. I visited my friends, their spouses, and their kids one family at a time, as if to catch up on missing out on the past two years. Then I ended up getting a job back at Medullan, the last company I'd worked for before my trip. Michael's rental place was available, so I settled there. A very relaxed, happy, and welcoming energy invigorated me. It felt right and comfortable to be back in the place I'd called home for seventeen years. Everything fell into place again.

Taipei truly had the magic power of rejuvenating me. After every visit, I became more extroverted. When I started at Cornell after my trip to Taipei, I made new friends without any problems. This time, after spending almost two years there, I was excited to see all my old friends. Rachel even commented, "You seem at your happiest right now." This was what being connected to my roots had done for me.

16

A ROMANTIC SCAM

After coming back to Boston from Taiwan, my life with friends and work settled back into place for about three and a half years. I'd been actively using OkCupid during this time and had gone on at least fifteen dates without any problems. I'd never met someone who intended to hurt me until I connected with a guy named Paul.

On July 7, 2018, I received a message from someone named Paul, who was forty-five and lived in New York City. I usually avoided meeting guys out of town, but Paul's kind manner in his photo caught my eye, and I made an exception. *New York is near Dad's,* I reasoned. The first message had substance: "I look forward to having meaningful conversations with you." I decided to respond, saying, "I like intimate conversations as well." He quickly asked, "How is online dating going for you? And what are you looking for? I'm looking for a woman who is ready for a serious long-term relationship with commitment. Would like to take each day at a time to learn more about you. How long have you been single? I got divorced almost four years ago, and I have a fifteen-year-old son who lives with me. I'm mentally and emotionally ready for something new." I thought, *Great, a man who knows what he wants: a real relationship.*

Paul was not shy. In an email, he wrote, "I'm originally from the Netherlands, and I've been living in the United States for almost thirteen years. I lived in California and Seattle until a few months before I moved to New York. I work as a project evaluator in disaster and aid management. I help to facilitate the distribution of relief aid and provide medical assistance to displaced people living in remote areas across the world. I've been doing it for seventeen years. It can be very challenging and rewarding."

He wanted to chat again the next day and asked when my birthday was. *My birthday? It's probably nothing, but I won't tell him. He's still a stranger.* He soon suggested we move off OkCupid, which seemed fast. It had only been three days since we first connected. He started checking in with good-morning and goodnight texts. Then he called me every night, which impressed my friends and me too.

Meanwhile, I started sharing more of my personal details with him. I told him my full name, my personal email address, and about my blog. Wanting to know more about him, I Googled him based on what I knew—his name, phone number, and email address—and found nothing at all. He had zero online presence, which I thought was unusual. I asked him if he used social media. He claimed he'd stopped using his Facebook profile during the Cambridge Analytica scandal when millions of pieces of Facebook data were used without permission for political advertising. But what about LinkedIn? As an independent consultant working for himself, he'd need a professional online presence.

In addition to messages, I asked Paul for pictures. He sent

me photos of his family, birthday party, and a camping trip. *Finally, photos!* I noticed there were pictures of two different campfires, one with large stones on the grass in front of a lake, while a second picture showed neat bricks staged in a small circle among crowded trees. One was very blurry. The other one seemed to be focusing on nothing. This seemed strange as they didn't look right or from places near each other, but I didn't ask about the discrepancy. *I am thinking too much. Perhaps he went to different places in one weekend.* I told him I now knew he was not a serial killer and that he was real. I sent him a few of my own recent photos and told him I was breaking my rule of no pictures before meeting in person.

He responded, "I'm not going to kill you with pictures!" I told him about my schizophrenia. He said he didn't mind.

Out of the blue, Paul told me he had deleted his profile on OkCupid and wanted to focus on us. I felt a shiver of uneasiness. But to reciprocate, I disabled mine the next day too.

On Monday, July 30, Paul happily told me he'd won the proposal he'd been working on, so he'd be employed for the next eighteen to twenty months. He announced it was time to come and see me. As I thought he was committing to getting to know me, I was happy to hear it. He said he'd let me know when we could meet.

A couple of days later, he explained he had to travel for work, hinting at not being able to visit. "Probably a couple of weeks. I'll email you my flight information." His itinerary showed flights from New York to Manila in the Philippines and from there to Boston. He did not book a flight leaving Boston to go back to New York, and I noticed the email looked oddly formatted.

While he was in Manila—because of the time-zone

difference—we talked less regularly. But he continued to make an effort to keep in touch. Then he started sharing details about his project and the financials. I again thought that was unusual.

Monday, August 20, 9:01 PM

Good morning, babe!
Hope you're having a wonderful day. Sorry I couldn't get to talk to you last night before going to bed. I had two separate meetings with the lawyers and the committee in charge of the legal process. We talked about the details surrounding the signing of the contract and the financial aspect from the budgeted capital, legal fees, and total accrued profit. In the end, I agreed to pay 8 percent of my total profit as the legal fee in advance, so the directors and the committee in charge can grant the lawyers the legal capacity to represent me in all the legal proceedings regarding the signing of the contract that binds the project approval, which is the final stage. I've written to my bank to make provisions for the legal fee, so we can proceed with the signing of the contract agreement.

Yesterday was the last meeting with the officials. Hopefully, the whole contract agreement will be finalized by tomorrow morning. It is a public holiday here today. I'll be spending most of today here at the apartment.

Talk to you before you go to bed.

Tuesday, August 20, 8:52 PM

Good evening to you!
Hope you've had a good day at work. I didn't have
to wake up at 1 a.m. for the phone call appointment
with the bank. I received an email in response to
my request for a short-term loan of $110,000.00 in
order to complete the payment for the legal fee. My
short-term loan request was denied, but they were
able to process the transfer of $260,000.00 as part
of the payment for the legal fee. As a result of this
disappointment, I won't be able to sign the contract
agreement until the end of the week while I look into
other options available for me to come up with the
remainder of the legal fees, which will take a few days.

I'm having a meeting at 9 a.m. with the directors
and the committee. I'm going to call you when I'm
through with the meeting.

I did the math. If 8 percent of his profit was $370,000,
Paul's profit for eighteen months was $4.6 million. That
seemed impossible for one person! I started having serious
doubts about him, thinking back on all these moments of
intuition when I felt something was a bit off about him.

For the rest of August, Paul worked on getting the funds
he needed to pay the lawyers. He got an additional thirty
thousand from his sister and parents and fifty thousand from
credit cards. He was still short by twenty thousand dollars.
If he did not have the money in a few days, he would lose the
whole project.

Meanwhile, different scenarios were running through my
head. I had a session with my therapist, Deborah. My gut told

me not to help him by lending him money. Deborah agreed and said, "Stay out of it." We both thought this could be a scam. But I held on to the belief that I'd met a good man and continued to hope for the best while promising Deborah I would be careful and protect myself.

Then over the weekend of August 30 to September 2, I didn't hear from Paul at all. I thought he might have lost his project and had started on his journey home to New York. *He must be devastated.* I did the math in my head and figured the project had been worth a couple of million. It was not like him not to communicate at all. I missed hearing from Paul and started worrying about him.

On Sunday night, September 2, Paul finally texted briefly. He was still in Manila and in the hospital. I was surprised and felt bad for him. His severe headaches had returned, which he went to the doctor for and told me about right before he traveled. It sounded serious. The deadline for his contract had been extended. On Tuesday, he texted again. He was not well enough to leave the hospital. On Thursday, September 6, Paul sent me this text:

I am not sure how you're going to feel about this, but I'm in a very difficult position regarding the whole legal agreement, and I'm not sure if there is something you can do to assist me financially. I want to know if you could at least lend me about $10,000 USD so as to be able to finalize the whole agreement. I'll be able to pay you back by the time I'm in New Jersey . . . thanks!

I texted back: "Paul, I just don't know you well enough to send money. It's a lot of money! How much are you short?"

Paul texted back, "I'm short about ten thousand." He specifically pointed out he was asking for American money.

I answered, "At this point, I am not comfortable lending you money. I only have your phone number. I don't even know your address. I am sorry."

"Okay. I understand. You don't have to be sorry."

"When is your new deadline?" I asked.

Paul texted, "Monday."

A day later, I wrote, "Any luck getting what you need?"

Paul replied, "No luck."

I asked, "Why would you have money in a week or two to pay me back but not right now? Also, what about your brother-in-law Sam, your friend in California, and other investment funds that you told me about? By the way, what is your address? Home address, I mean."

No answer.

"So does this mean that you are not going to get this project? What's happening on Monday? I think this whole thing is a bit crazy, especially that you are doing this all on your own and don't have a team of people with you."

I sent Paul a list of banks that offer short-term loans with 6.99 to 24.99 APR and asked, "How much money do you already have? Would these people really reject a selected vendor for ten thousand? Does not make any sense to me!"

Paul replied, "I'm sorry, but I wouldn't have asked you for help if I wasn't going to lose out completely on this project. There wouldn't be any reason for me to do what I did." I thought he was talking about asking me for money.

I texted, "It could be a scam. You could disappear. I have no idea, no way of knowing."

Then he was gone.

I oscillated between trusting Paul and being cautious since

I'd never met the man. I didn't want my imagination to get ahead of me.

A sure sign of trouble was how quickly the conversations turned to money matters. The business arrangement he described didn't make sense. I didn't understand what he did for a living, as much as it sounded noble. Why would he not have anyone but a stranger to ask for money? Why would he be so short of cash if he could bid on such a large project? Why was he not better prepared for his contract negotiation? He certainly didn't manage his business and money well.

A week after Paul stopped texting and calling me, I shared the story with my close friends. They validated my suspicions. We all agreed this had been a romantic scam—a very elaborate one that lasted two months! "Paul Henriks" from New York probably did not exist. There might even be a team of people. This was their work, and I was their project. This could happen to anyone!

"I'm so glad you didn't fall for this guy. Horrible," Rachel said.

A few friends sent me online articles of other romantic scams. They all followed a similar pattern. Initially, the men were very nice, almost perfect. But all of a sudden, some dramatic emergency happened: maybe a health scare, maybe a work-related event. But there was always something to trigger the need for emergency help in the form of money. Then the men disappeared.

I reported Paul to OkCupid, and they responded right away. His profile and our messages were deleted, but I asked Rachel and Michael if OkCupid could prevent scammers from doing that sort of thing again. After all, he could just create another new profile in five minutes. It didn't seem like a real solution, but maybe they could do more behind the scenes.

As predicted, about six months or so later, I saw the same polished profile picture online again with a different name, stating the man was from Texas. Rachel suggested I file a police report, and I went to the police station. Because nothing had happened to me, there was nothing they could do.

Needless to say, I was much more guarded after this. Every time I saw a glossy profile picture, I had the same immediate thought: *Maybe this is another scammer.*

17

THE WALL OF STICKIES

One sunny day as I walked down Newbury Street, feeling glad that the scam was behind me and content about having spent almost two years in Taipei, I remembered a conversation I'd had with a female therapist in her living room ten years before. In my early thirties at the time, I wasn't aware of my exact mental condition, but trying to sort through my thoughts, I decided to talk to a therapist. I asked Michael for help, and he said a professional might be more helpful than he could be and referred me to someone he really liked to talk to. Because Michael recommended her, I optimistically decided to give her a try.

Susan was my first therapist. I wasn't sure how she could help me, but I wanted to talk to someone about what was on my mind. We met at her house in the South End. She lived on the same street as Chris. It was the first time I'd been back to our old—or Chris's—neighborhood.

When I rang the doorbell, she opened the door. Susan was a tall, handsome Caucasian woman. Confident, calm, with short curly hair. She owned many cats, more than three for sure.

"Come in," she said. I followed her to a room with a sofa and chairs, some occupied by her cats. Good thing I wasn't allergic. "Make yourself comfortable. Sit anywhere you like."

I sat down on the left side of the sofa, and she sat in a chair right next to me. She asked me about my parents and work. After I finished telling her everything worth mentioning, she looked me straight in the eye and asked, "What do you like to do?"

I thought about this for a second. As a thirtysomething, I'd never really asked myself that question.

"Ice skating." I immediately added, "But I don't do much of it. I'm not sure why."

Susan gave me a reassuring smile. "When you go home, I want you to find a blank wall in your apartment. Get a stack of stickies. Write on each sticky paper what you like to do and put them all up on the wall. The more, the better. You can see them all every day."

Then our time together was up. I made three more appointments with her but didn't find her helpful when it came to clearing up my confusion about schizophrenia, which I was unable to be upfront about. At that time, I didn't know how to talk about it. Then I stopped seeing her and quickly forgot about most of our conversations.

Ten years later, I remembered that first meeting on the way home. I wasn't sure how many stickies I would have. I never put up that wall of stickies. I didn't need to. I'd just started dating and was getting to know myself through my conversations with single men. But Susan's words often flashed through my mind. I realized that in my head, I had an invisible wall with many stickies. Over the years, I slowly checked them off one by one. Travel would go on a sticky. Actually, the different countries I visited would go on different stickies. Different writing projects. Spending time with family and friends. Being there when they needed help. Dinner with Rachel, Wendy, and others. Working in different positions at different companies. Books I read or wanted to read. Restaurants I tried or wanted to try. Concerts and plays. The stickies would go on and on.

I no longer thought of having nothing to put on the wall, and I no longer had nothing to say about what I love to do.

Instead of stickies, when I looked around my home, I saw meaningful personal items all over. In my dining room, two vertical magnetic boards brimmed with magnets collected from my travels. Between them hung a larger board with strings, where I hung holiday cards recently received. I could see the smiling faces of different families in my life. In my living room hung a painting from Santorini on a piece of beautiful, irregularly shaped wood showing the iconic view of white houses on a cliff during a beautiful sunset. The sunset shone on the turquoise sea. Small statues from Italy, Peru, Mexico, and Russia stood on either side of the painting. In another area, two small framed pictures graced the wall: one of a hill in Acapulco, hand-painted, and the other of the Eiffel Tower, a digital photo. On the adjacent wall, in the center, a precious black-and-white picture taken on January 1, 1950 of my grandparents and their children. Surrounding that were pictures of friends.

I'd found my center in Taiwan and finally felt right at home in Boston.

— Part 3 —

MATURE

18

DATING IN MY FORTIES

Dating as a fortysomething was not much better than it was in my twenties or thirties. Instead of meeting someone in person, I looked at a profile for style, posture, and height. Age was no longer a question but was clearly labeled next to his name. Rachel had told me from the start that profile photos mattered. To me, a profile including photos showed how much effort someone was willing to put into dating, so those pictures and his bio and description with it worked as a first impression, though it certainly didn't tell the *whole* story about a person. I still had to ask questions to get to know someone. I liked to ask three basic ones when I first talked to a man: Where were you born? Where did you go to school? What do you do for work? That way, I got a sense of someone's background, where he'd been in the world and in terms of experience, and where he might be headed.

From the first messages to the first couple of dates, I experienced what I called dating episodes and sent synopses to Rachel and Michael, my close friends, also known as my dating support group.

DATING EPISODES

July 6, 2016
Dear Friends,
Here are a few more recent natural deaths of
initial encounters.

Condition: Initial encounter with Daniel
Status: Died of a natural conversation
Cause of death: Harry Potter
Notes: Can he have a problem with reading? Really?
Wow.

Condition: Initial encounter with Josh
Status: Died of a natural conversation
Cause of death: Slow texting about boring topics
Notes: He's very cute! We have a high percentage of
matchness. That made our total number of messages
extend from single digitals to double. But death was
inevitable regardless of how good-looking he was
because he was *boring*.

Condition: First look at Mark's profile
Status: Happily married and looking for more
Cause of death: Speechless
Notes: I know these things happen, but it's still
shocking when I run into these normal-looking men
with different values. Why do they think there are
women out there who want to help them cheat on
their wives?

Condition: Initial encounter with Stephen
Status: Quick natural death
Cause of death: Eagerness to meet immediately
instead of getting to know each other a bit more first.

We didn't even have a good conversation. "Can we meet now?" "Can we meet now?" "Can we meet NOW!" Ugh.

Condition: First date with an older Italian from Venice
Status: Two goodbye kisses, one on each cheek
Cause of death: Inactivity in my brain. Zero chemistry or fun, even though it was one of the worldliest conversations I've ever had on a date. Traveling to different cities. Experiencing different cultures and cuisines. Meeting people around the globe. But the good thing is that I finally experienced the worldliness that I had in my head about Europeans. It's blah alright.
    Notes: FYI, did you know that the Nespresso Café near Taj is a European hangout? More than half of the people there speak in foreign languages.

Condition: Saying goodbye to a forceful kisser
Status: Wiping off my lips and walking away
Cause: The two of us walked out of a bakery and stood in front of each other to say goodbye. I was not expecting it, but he forced a kiss on the lips. I was taken aback and didn't feel any gentleness or caring. He wanted to show me that he was interested. But I was not.

"LOL!!!!!!!!!!!!!!!!!!!!!!!!!!!!!!!!!" Rachel saw my humor in these failed starts.
    "Especially funny was 'Speechless.' Glad his name wasn't my husband's! ;-)"
    "I like this format of summarizing the potential mates. Very witty!"

"Glad to hear you're taking it in stride :) The most important thing is that you're happy."

"These updates are hysterical. Shows how many wrongs are out there, which will make finding the right one more worthwhile."

Michael said at one point, "These men don't have a chance. They don't know you have an army behind you!" Even though single, I was not dating alone. I felt safe and supported and had fun and lots of good laughs.

The very first online date I had when I was forty-one seemed novel. But with more experience, dating became enjoyable. I learned to make quick yes-or-no decisions online. I responded to messages optimistically and imperfectly. My mind did its magical calculation of all the factors important to me, hesitantly at first and then more confidently.

I learned my first impression based on an online profile was hit or miss. Zach wore sunglasses in his profile picture. I was surprised by how he actually looked, much older and less cool when I met him in person. Everyone put up their best pictures and bios. Words and pictures didn't tell everything. What was not said or shown might be equally important. I learned to expect surprises during these first dates. I made a list in my head to use when I was perusing potential matches online: Don't rely only on sunglass photos. Face and full-body picture required. No mention of "open relationship" or "dating with a serious girlfriend." No repeated selfies in the bathroom. No repeated bare-chest gym photos. No burning flag or book. I was learning to understand how to translate online imagery to qualities I desired in men. The same thinking also applied to the rest of the profile and initial interactions. A man who was chatty via text messages might not be talkative in person.

His profile might've said he was looking for a long-term relationship, but he didn't have time in reality to meet.

Remember Adam, the man who stood me up at the Publick House? I had waited for two hours alone, all dressed up while eating that tasteless garden burger. When I woke up the next day, I felt betrayed. I wasn't sure if I should be upset or dismissive. I was feeling both. I didn't want to do either. I felt hurt by someone with whom I had been texting for weeks yet had never met. I wanted to know why he didn't show. I didn't want to judge. I traced my steps and wrote to my friends.

He'd said he was going home to sleep at around nine or ten on Wednesday morning after he'd left the fire station. That was the last time I'd heard from him. While I was at the Publick House that night, I texted him "Are you sleeping?" as sort of a joke.

When I came home from the Publick House, I checked OkCupid briefly, and he appeared to be online—there was a little green dot next to his name. *Was he checking the dating website while I was waiting alone at the restaurant?* When I still didn't receive any text by nine that night, I went to bed.

The next morning, I saw several texts from him from around 2 to 4 a.m. on Thursday, saying he'd been asleep and he was "so, so sorry." I texted back at around 9 a.m.: "What happened?"

"I didn't wake up until two in the morning," he said. He expected me to believe he went to bed at 10 a.m. and slept through the day and night until two the next morning.

Continuing on with our texting, Adam said he'd had a long and rough shift (his shift was on Monday, and it ended on Tuesday at 8 a.m.) and was putting out a fire. I wanted very much to believe him, but his story didn't add up. Several texts later, I wanted to see what he really thought about meeting up, so I texted, "Do you want to try to meet again?" I hadn't heard back from him since I asked. Obviously, he didn't want to meet. I shouldn't have suggested that we meet no matter how much I wanted to do so. I needed to let him decide that he wanted to meet.

I tried to guess his reasons for not showing up. Reason one: He'd slept through our date and hadn't bothered to use an alarm clock or text to cancel. Reason two: He forgot about our date. Reason three: He didn't feel like coming. Whatever it was, it seemed irresponsible, and I was glad I hadn't already gotten more involved with him. *How many more dinners would I have been eating alone if we'd gotten together? Do I want to be with a man who is not communicative? Do I want to live with frequent disappointments?*

Texting was a critical part of the online dating experience. It replaced talking as the standard method of the first contact between potential mates. Initial texts usually gave me an idea of what the person was like, for instance, if his behavior was normal or not and if there were any early signs of incompatibility. I hadn't had any negative feelings about Adam in the beginning, but I was not interested in being someone's text buddy. Furthermore, a person's texting personality could be misleading and might not be representative of the actual person—again, like Adam. I know I have a creative imagination and might infer what someone might be like through their texts. As Rachel said, the real deal is still meeting up to actually get to know a person.

Adam did the worst ghosting to me, but he was not the only one. Many other guys flaked out during initial texting or after the first or second date. I hit it off with Quan, a furnituremaker, during our first date when we met for a light dinner at a tapas place near my place. This was followed by a second date at the beach and exploring a local bookstore. After two dates, I texted him, and he never responded.

Confused about the situation, I chatted with Michael about being ghosted by men. "He's gotta show up," he said. It didn't matter how much I liked the guy and thought we had fun texting, drinking coffee, having dinner, or being at the beach. In order to start something, the man needed to want to text, call, or meet up. It's not what they say; it's what they do. I should look at a man's behaviors to tell whether or not he's engaged and interested. If there isn't any action, I can't ignore it or look for reasons. It just means that he's not my man.

That was why I thought I might have better success with Dorothy, the matchmaker, because the men she found for me were screened carefully and should be just as invested as I was in finding the right partner.

I met Victor through Dorothy as another blind date. She sent another bio about a potential match: "Victor is a researcher and doctor, divorced ten years ago. He has a passion for cooking and trying new foods. He loves to play around in the kitchen. He's well-mannered and polished but not stuffy. He has three children and is very close with them. His youngest daughter is still at home, and he enjoys cooking with her. They recently went to a cooking class together. He's looking for someone open-minded and adventurous."

I arrived at the restaurant first and waited for him at our table. Victor was on time, well-dressed, and friendly, slim, Asian, and classy. He greeted me with a nice smile and a soft-spoken hello. We sat across from each other.

It turned out Victor worked at Massachusetts General

Hospital, one of the most prestigious hospitals in the United States, and researched at MIT. When he arrived, I realized I had seen his profile and pictures on OkCupid as well. He also had a connection to Taiwan. He told me right away he didn't like the restaurant Dorothy had suggested and picked this Taiwanese restaurant, Jo Jo Taipei, in Allston instead after she told him about me.

There were about ten tables in Jo Jo Taipei, and we were the only two people there. Victor was clearly in touch with both his American and Taiwanese cultural sides to suggest having a date in a little, authentic, and unassuming joint that only local Taiwanese would visit. I decided that was a super plus. *I like him already!*

I ordered a supersonic—Bully Boy Gin, Génépy, honey, and Mediterranean tonic—while Victor ordered a cognac. He passionately launched our conversation right into the cancer research work that he was conducting at MIT. At a crossroad in his career, Victor was trying to figure out if he should stay in medicine or academia—or do both if he could continue to handle it. He actively mentored students and did so many interesting things, and he wanted to do more. He impressed me. Better yet, he showed interest in my career and my passions. I told him about my work and writing. We talked for a couple of hours. The waiters came by and took orders for our second drinks.

We spent another couple of hours talking about interesting places in the world. He traveled quite a bit. Then we mixed travel talk with food talk. We both loved food. He knew all the local places I liked. He obviously had a very good memory and told me lots of fun details.

When I told Victor I wanted to take a sailing trip to Croatia, he asked if I knew why people liked Croatia as a travel destination. I wasn't sure what he meant by that question. Why would I care about whether or not other people wanted to go to the same place I did? Then he laughed and said, "It's because of *Game of Thrones*." That wasn't why I wanted to go there, but I let that go.

I really liked that he knew all the Taiwanese dishes that I knew. "Which dish do you like the best?" he asked.

"Scallion jellyfish." I'd not had it in a while since I didn't usually go to Taiwanese restaurants on my own.

The time went by quickly, and suddenly it was almost 10 p.m. When we finished our meal, he asked if I wanted to stop by the pastry store, which was something I always did with my friends and family after a meal in Chinatown. Victor felt so familiar in some ways.

At the end of the evening, I thanked him for picking up the bill. He gave me his number. "I'd like to see you again," he said, completely disregarding Dorothy's protocol again.

I told him that I was taking the T home, and he walked me to the stop. As I sat alone on the train on my way home, I felt torn. *I really like him, but I have a simple life. Would someone with so many things going on be a good match for me? Could he do nothing on a Saturday, just sit next to me and be happy?*

When Dorothy called, I thanked her for finding such a quality date. I was happy and cautiously optimistic. I had already shared the details of my date with Rachel and Michael, who were happy for me. Victor was the type of man I wanted to meet, someone who had his life together.

Typically, after each blind date that Dorothy set up for me, she would call me on the phone, and we would discuss how it went. I'd tell her if I wanted to see the person again and if there was anything I wanted to adjust.

I sat comfortably on my sofa with a cup of iced coffee in Brookline while she was in Nantucket. "Great find. I had a great time meeting Victor last night. We had a lot to discuss, and somehow we ended up talking about big things that we want to do in life—things we care about plus things we love. He's obviously smart and articulate. At the same time, he's friendly and open to my ideas. I like his personality. He was very interesting, and it was a great date. And I think he is good-looking! As far as how I feel about seeing him again—" I took a breath because I knew she was waiting for that. "I'm not going to have any expectations at this point. He sounds pretty busy. It's too early to think about developing a relationship after just one date. I'm more patient now, I think. I'll let what may come, come." I cheerfully said, "So, yes, I would like to see him again."

Dorothy nodded. "I'm so glad you enjoyed your date with Victor. He did as well. Sounds like you have a new partner for checking out new food spots. I love that you're taking the approach of enjoying getting to know someone as a friend. Who knows where something could lead? I think Victor will be great for you to test out some of the things you've learned in order to allow your dating journey to unfold naturally without the pressure of wanting a relationship. He liked that you're very open and have an open mind and loves that you're up to try new things and challenge him. Since this is a yes/yes match, I'll do the number exchange for you both. Victor's number is (xxx) xxx-xxxx."

A couple of days later, I texted Victor to say hello. He didn't respond for a few days. I waited and then texted again: "Hi, good morning. On my way to DC at the airport. Pretty quiet. Want to ping you one last time. Have you lost interest? Let me know."

Victor responded, "Hope you are enjoying DC. Did you make it to Rose's Luxury? I apologize I've been lapse in getting back to you because I've been traveling quite a bit. In fact, I'm traveling again to Orlando this weekend through the midweek and then to New York City. For now, I seem to be too busy to pursue a further romantic interest, but I'm open to checking in occasionally and maybe going to dinner sometime."

I wrote, "Hi! Now getting a text from you is a bit of a surprise! I did not get to Rose's. Busy week in DC. I had a workshop all day yesterday. Sure, I would be open to keeping in touch. Safe travels! Don't burn yourself out. P.S. Thanks for being clear. I do appreciate that."

He replied, "Thank you. Take care."

What? I felt hurt, disappointed, and rejected. *If he doesn't have time, why did he agree to the date? What a waste of everyone's time.*

I came up with reasons Victor couldn't meet. Of course, I hoped for the best whenever I met someone. Here I was again, trying to explain *his* behavior and to make myself feel better. In this case, I could say, "He's very busy as a doctor. He's saving lives." But his behavior really said that I was not a priority in his life. Maybe dating was not even a priority for him. It could be that dating for him came after work, kids, social commitments, and more. He could indeed be very busy with other responsibilities. Regardless, it was a decision he made. If a man wasn't willing to spend time and energy getting to know me, there would be no future for us. I found that if something or someone was important, I could always find the time.

I emailed Dorothy and told her that Victor was too busy. Expectations were tough. No one was perfect, including me. When I met someone, I filtered him based on prerequisites I'd figured out over time. Dorothy did the same for me. During our first meeting, she had told me that I had to prioritize my criteria. She said, "It's unrealistic to look for everything." So I started with the foundation of having the same life values. The priorities that I shared with Dorothy were positive energy, passion, intelligence, open-mindedness (to different cultures and backgrounds), and a direction in life. Chemistry was also important to me. For example, kindness was a requirement, but living in Boston was optional. In such cases, some give and take is good.

Dorothy and I had never talked about availability. It seemed that with every blind date she set up for me, I found more expectations that I didn't tell her but were a given to me. Dorothy wanted to know if I could quantify the amount of time I wanted to spend with my partner. "Sounds like you need someone around more. If I am screening someone and they travel, what sort of questions would you like me to ask to make sure it's a good fit (i.e., how many days in a month or year)?" It seemed impossible for me to let her know my every single thought.

Victor and I never went on a second date. I had hoped that he would text me after we were both back in town. Since I left it to him, time just went on, and by the time I thought of him again, it was a year or so later. *Whatever happened to Victor?* I messaged him, and he didn't respond. *I don't blame him. In his busy life, I didn't make a strong enough impression and was never a priority for him.*

"Why was he asked to have a date with you if he didn't have time to date you? Shouldn't that be part of the screening?" Rachel wouldn't let this go.

"But I didn't say anything about how much time I wanted from a man. There could be so many different kinds of relationships."

"I wonder where she found him. Doesn't make sense."

I soon discovered that the men Dorothy set up for me might not be as invested in meeting someone as serious as I was about having a real relationship. Anyone could be my date, both paying FindLove clients like me or someone not using the service at all. Rachel pointed out to me that this was not a good thing and that the power balance between the two people was off from the start because I was paying a premium for something that was apparently free of charge to my date. Having a matchmaker wasn't better for everything, so I continued to date on my own.

When I first met Sam on OkCupid, I said to my friends, "The good news is I want to share what Sam messaged me this week. Sam is Japanese American. He's skinnier than I am, but I don't hold that against him. He writes perfectly in complete sentences and coherent paragraphs. He's handsome, works on space satellites, grew up in Massachusetts, owns his own place, and lives in Cambridge. Even though we've only been messaging back and forth, the messages are filled with substance. We're planning to meet this coming Saturday after message number twelve! He likes hiking and biking and asked if I would be interested in a few less challenging trails. Oh, and he went to Cornell. :-)"

I was excited because Sam and I had both mentioned *The Martian* on our profiles as our favorite film, plus we had the Cornell connection. I had suggested we meet at one of my favorite places, Café Fixe, at 2 p.m. on Saturday. Before meeting, I looked again at his profile and photos, feeling very hopeful.

On Saturday, I spent more time than usual thinking about what to wear. Dressing up made me happy, partly for me and not just for him. Since I still had extra time, I straightened my hair. I liked dating in the summer because I could wear my favorite sundress and cute sandals. I didn't have any expectations for the first date but felt excited. The world was full of possibilities.

Sam arrived on time, a quality I cared about but didn't demand. He looked handsome and neat and seemed friendly. His photos were true to life. He offered to buy me coffee, and I let him. Café Fixe was a small and cozy place. We sat on wooden chairs in front of a window, facing each other. The sun shone. We couldn't stop talking to each other for the entire afternoon. We started with Cornell, then the movie *The Martian*, and then on to personal questions about work, family, and hobbies. He obviously cared very much about his family and felt passionate about his work. I didn't keep track of the time; it went by so quickly.

Sam checked his watch. We were both surprised that three hours had passed. "What would you like to do now?" he asked.

"I could eat," I said, still having a good time. Mentally, I was ignoring one of Rachel's golden rules: Keep the first date short. It should be in and out.

"I know this nice little family restaurant in Coolidge Corner. Want to go there for dinner?" he asked.

So we continued our first date and had dinner at a Japanese restaurant. This was the longest first date I'd ever had. Needless to say, we liked each other. We ended the date by agreeing that we'd see each other again and waved goodbye at a distance.

For our next few dates, we went to the Arnold Arboretum and Charles River and walked the rest of Boston, which, on one date, ended up being more than ten miles. After the walk, we went for Thai in Back Bay. We then spent another couple of full days being with and talking to each other. Our curiosity about each other was contagious—we asked questions and gave answers. Hanging out with Sam felt so natural. When we weren't together, we exchanged long emails and photos of our families and daily lives. He felt traditional that way, like when people still wrote letters on paper. I loved that about him and us.

Mentally, I had a plan. Chat messages. First date. Second date. Get to know about his work, then family, and then past relationships. Invite him to my place so he can see that I am a minimalist. Visit his place to see what his place is like. The list went on and on. I felt Sam and I were making great progress getting to know each other; we had gone the furthest since I started dating again. Most men I met didn't make it past the first or second date.

On a weeknight, Sam got us tickets to Roxane Gay's book reading and picked me up. As much as I loved books, I'd never been to an author reading before. A long line curved around the entrance to the auditorium in Cambridge High School. Sam and I were the last few to get seated. Luckily, he'd found two seats together on the left side toward the back. I enjoyed seeing Roxane and realized she was pretty funny. The reading lasted about ninety minutes.

Sitting in that auditorium with Sam, I felt like a college student waiting to soak in every word the author said. "Isn't she great?" Sam whispered to me.

"Yes, amazing."

Afterward, Sam asked, "What do you want to do next? Where should we go?"

"I can still hang out a bit. There are a few cafés in Washington Square near me. Maybe that would be the easiest?"

Sam parked his car, and we walked across the street to Caffé Nero. Even though the lights were on, there was no one inside.

"Oh, it's closed," Sam said. I checked the time. It was a bit after 9 p.m. "How about going to my place? You can meet my cat," he continued.

"Hm. I think it's late. I should really go home. Thank you for a wonderful night."

"Are you sure? My cat is really cute and cuddly."

"Yes, I'm sure."

On our fourth date, Sam came over to my apartment, and I cooked dinner for us. To me, this was a big deal, even though I didn't show it. It was the first time since Chris that I had invited a man to my place for dinner. What I didn't know at the time was that when a woman made such an invitation, she was giving the sign that she wanted something more intimate to happen. I didn't have kissing or cuddling in mind, and I rarely initiated physical intimacy. All I wanted was to cook him a nice meal.

He helped out, having brought some of the ingredients I needed like fresh scallions and garlic, cherry tomatoes, and eggs. I prepared a couple of simple Taiwanese dishes that were my personal favorites: scrambled eggs with tomatoes and fried rice sticks. Sam liked them and ate a good amount. Because I was trying to be a good host, it was hard for me to focus on Sam completely. I wanted to make him comfortable and made sure he had everything he needed. "Is the food okay?" "Do you need more water?" I wanted everything to be perfect.

After dinner, he wanted to show me pictures of his family. I loved that. He took out his iPad. Without thinking too much, we sat on opposite ends of my sofa, so there was a lot of space between us. He showed me who was whom. When it got late, I told him I had a great night. Looking a bit quiet, he said goodbye, waved his hands, and then left in a hurry. I got the impression he was slightly frustrated but quickly dismissed it.

On our fifth date, I went to his place, and he gave me a tour of his home, which was a one-bedroom apartment in a brick building on a quiet street. I met his cat, a tabby. She was rubbing against my legs. I liked his fish tank. It was big and very clean. I remembered the fish tank my dad had when I was little. It took effort to keep it so clean and filled with healthy plants. He told me that he renovated the bathroom and removed the tub. He was also a neat person, with everything in its color-coordinated place. Things were going along well when all of a sudden, he sat down on his sofa with a sad face.

"I want to talk to you about something," he said.

"Uh-oh," I reacted to his seriousness.

"I don't know if this," he pointed to him and then to me, "will work. Do you feel butterflies?"

I didn't know what to say. Maybe, "I was hoping you would hold my hand when we were walking our ten miles together," but I was too shy to bring that up. "Okay, I guess I should go home. Would you give me a ride?"

"Yes, of course."

Sam was nice, but he was right. He could be a great friend. We might have been attracted to each other intellectually, but we didn't experience butterflies. We'd kept our hands to ourselves. I felt that I had gotten ahead of myself when I thought we might have more of a future together.

Sam and I continued to email after that conversation. Soon after our last date, he sent me this email:

> Hi Mindy, I went to Porter Square this morning to check out a store run by local artists, hoping to buy some handmade pottery or jewelry as gifts for my family; nothing caught my eye, but I did finally get to enjoy my ramen by getting in line at a restaurant opening. Visited my parents and helped assemble a riding vehicle for the three-year-old and caught up with my folks. My sister came by, so I was asking her advice about relationships from a woman's point of view. I saw your text and am glad that you are going to date other guys. I do enjoy your company and do hope that we can be and remain friends.

I needed to talk to Rachel because I didn't know what I wanted to do in this situation. Sam was a decent man, and I wanted it to work out romantically. I liked him and was disappointed that it didn't. It felt easier to just stop talking to him. I didn't want to put myself in a position to have any hope for something that wouldn't happen. I decided to protect myself. So this how I responded:

> Hi Sam, After some more thought, I don't think I am interested in being friends. It's confusing to me since we met on OkCupid. I think it would be best to cancel going to Blue Hills together on Saturday. If

you ever want to go on a date again, you know how
to find me. Best of luck with dating and looking for
the right girl! I wish you the very best.

It was hard to decide and say this, but Rachel was proud
of me. About a year later, I texted him to say hello. He told me
that he had a girlfriend. I was glad for him but disappointed
for me. I had wondered if we might have a second chance. Sam
was a good guy. That was our last message to each other.

Regarding Sam, Rachel's advice was "Don't forget to enjoy
the journey. Next time, don't do too much too quickly."

I planned—that was what I did for a living. It was very
easy and natural for me to think of the next fifty steps after
meeting someone. I treated Sam like a good friend and
planned from the very start. It was clear in my mind. I was
satisfied that everything was going according to my plan. But
we had gotten to our fifth date when he finally said, "I don't
feel any connection."

After this experience, instead of concentrating on making
progress and checking things off a list, I learned to slow down.
Don't get ahead of yourself. Take it one day at a time. I needed
to enjoy getting to know someone and focus on the person.
Without some kind of connection or attraction, everything
else mattered very little. I needed to be in touch not just with
our brains but our hearts.

The day before my forty-fifth birthday, I met Rudy via
Tinder. He was a divorced dad with two daughters. The older
girl was sociable but did not get good grades. The younger one
was more particular and academically smart. He went to the
gym twice a week, lifting weights. He worked at a software
company and traveled professionally. The year before, he'd

traveled to about twenty cities, including business trips, and he loved it.

He seemed sweet and considerate and loved traveling and live music. He told me he'd just found out about a twelve-hour train ride through Alaska with amazing views. We both thought it sounded romantic. We exchanged photos of our hard-earned travel magnets on our fridges. He grew up sailing up and down the coastal islands in New England and around the islands of Maine. He read. In addition to being a dad to his own girls, he tried to be a father figure for his nephew whose parents were also divorced.

We had two dates and laughed almost the whole time during both. At some point, I told him about my first book and that it was about schizophrenia. His response was "Oh, everyone has something unusual in their family. My dad's side is full of people with mental anxieties about one thing or another." He was sure he had something going on mentally or emotionally too. I felt both relieved and dismayed by his response. I liked him, but I wasn't sure about wanting to develop something with a man who was twice divorced, smoked weed, and worked out all the time to release stress and anxiety. I found myself holding back, but I was not sure why since I thought he was great in other ways.

As we finished up our second date, we agreed that we wanted to see each other again after my return from a trip to Aruba with my girlfriend Jasmine. A day later, I texted him first and told him what I was doing that week, suggesting we go to Club Passim for our third date. There was no response, and I sensed something was wrong. So I texted him again. After a few pleasantries, I got right to the point: "Is something wrong?"

He confessed, "I don't think we are a good match." I was so surprised. I hadn't seen this coming at all. We were just making plans.

"Why, may I ask?"

"I feel like you are pursuing me rather than the other way around."

I didn't take that well. I never thought I had come across as pushy or aggressive. He didn't say those words, but I felt they were implied. Here I was again, doing too much too quickly, just like I did with Sam.

I talked to Rachel and Michael right away. "He thinks I'm pushy. I can't believe that's how I'm coming across." I considered myself to be the most laidback person among my friends.

"Guys like to lead, Mindy. You shouldn't have texted him first," Rachel said.

"I thought we were over that phase." I felt slightly hurt.

"You texted him first. Then you planned the date. Men don't like that."

"I was just trying to be helpful." But based on what happened, Rachel's theory seemed on point.

"If you're in a relationship already, then it doesn't matter. But you are not," she continued.

"I think it depends on the guy," Michael chimed in.

"Well, if he really likes you, it wouldn't matter anyway. So that's not really the point," Rachel said.

"If I like someone, I want to do something about it," I said. If I didn't care about this guy, I would have done nothing. Couldn't he see that?

I ended up agreeing with Rachel. Getting extra attention from me, in that I had texted him right away, wouldn't have been a negative feeling if he had liked me more. I realized that it was hard for me to stay neutral toward any man I dated. To me, either I liked him, or I didn't. If I liked someone, I wanted to let him know. But Rudy told me directly that I was "too much." My MO obviously didn't work for him.

I finally met a man with whom sexual chemistry blossomed from the start. We connected via OkCupid. Then Peter and I met at Tatte, and I led him to Hourly Oyster to continue our conversation. We immediately felt comfortable with each other, sharing stories about our love for food. I laughed a lot and found him funny and attractive. What a great smile. He kept telling me I was "so hot." He definitely wanted to take me home with him. At last: a balanced date with both mental and physical attraction. We messed around a bit in his car. Right after the date, he asked me out again. So fun and easy.

We made plans for a second date. I showed up at the restaurant first, and when he arrived, we both smiled at each other. He took my hands and said, "I won't be able to look at you and eat dinner with you. Let's go." I felt the physical connection as well and decided to go home with him. I'd wanted to explore having sex with him, and Peter made me feel excited about going for it. We had fun at his place, mostly in his bedroom. I made sure he used a condom. Everything escalated very quickly, and we both enjoyed it.

I put men in two different categories when it comes to how they act after we have sex. One type of man wants to cuddle and hug. I still remember the first time a man put his arm around me after we finished. I felt the tenderness in his embrace as we both lay in bed. The other type was Peter, who lay in bed quietly, deep in his own thoughts, enjoying by himself what he had just done.

After leaving the bedroom, he offered me a glass of red

wine in his living room, but he didn't want to talk about anything. He just sat there. I didn't disturb him but checked out his place in companionable silence. Then he offered to drop me off at home.

When I texted him over the weekend, he told me I might have the wrong idea about what had happened between the two of us. "I don't want a relationship right now," he said. I was confused and surprised. I thought we'd hit it off. Okay, he just wanted to have fun for one night. On his profile, he said he was looking for a relationship. *What the hell?* However, I was not mentally invested in him like I was with Sam, with whom I talked and emailed for a while. *I also had a fun night, not just him. He doesn't owe me anything at this point.* I guess I just had a one-night stand. Another first.

Rachel was livid. "What? He's in his forties, and he doesn't want a relationship? He'll never be ready if he still doesn't know what he wants."

I moved on.

I really liked Ted from up north. Ted had "super liked" me on Tinder. Immediately, we started texting each other nonstop with lots of flirting and joking. I felt the chemistry, and so did he. I was so distracted by him that I couldn't focus on work—a first for me.

One morning, he texted saying he was in the area and asked if I could meet up. I was on the T on my way into work. "Now? Today?" He had taken a ski trip over the weekend and was on his way back to New Hampshire. He wanted to stop by to see me. I told him he'd have to come to me since I was headed into work and couldn't really go far to anywhere else. But I wanted to see him and make it work. I left work at ten and met up with him at Sofra Bakery and Café. He was as cute

in person as in his photo. We chatted for twenty minutes, and
then I had to leave. After that, we continued to text throughout
the days and into the nights. He came to see me near work
again a few days later. We were into each other, as can be seen
from the following texts:

"Hi. I was thinking. Would you be open to coming up to
visit me over the weekend? We can see each other between
my shifts at the ER. And I don't have the boys this weekend,"

"Sure. I don't mind."

"Okay. I think there is a bus here from Boston. It's for an
hour. I can pick you up."

"That sounds easy enough."

We spent most of our time together in his bedroom.
Glorious. I hadn't spent time with a man like that in years.
I visited him in Portsmouth over a few more consecutive
weekends since my schedule was more flexible than his. I
was accommodating and easygoing. I also made it clear to
Ted that I wanted outside time as much as bedroom time. He
took me to nearby restaurants for brunches and dinners when
he wasn't working at the ER as an anesthesiologist. While he
worked, I kept busy enjoying his picturesque New England
town near the water. I enjoyed our time together during his
breaks between shifts. I didn't mind doing what I could to
make it work.

Rachel, however, had a different perspective. "You just met
him! Why are you the one going up there all the time? Why
doesn't he come down to see you? Why should you be the one
making all the effort?"

I thought about this. *Do I feel that I am being taken advantage of?* No, I didn't. I liked him, and I felt that he liked me.

During one of my weekends in New Hampshire, Ted

had a completely free twenty-four hours, which almost never happened. I didn't expect what he suggested. "Can we go car shopping?"

"Okay." That didn't sound romantic, but I went along. After all, he had limited free time and needed a new car. As we stood at a car dealer, Ted talked to the salesman while I waited, which didn't feel good, but I pretended to be okay with it. I went along. I felt the impact of how he'd decided to spend his precious free time later, and I could feel my disappearance beginning to creep in—like how I felt with Chris at the end of our relationship.

After I came home and had some time with myself, I thought about how we'd spent our only free day together at a car dealership, where he mostly focused on cars. I was not happy about that. So why did I let it happen? Why did I tell him I was okay with that? I didn't think voicing my opinion to Ted posed a problem. Or would it? *Maybe my personality is not suited to a love relationship. Maybe I am too laidback to have a man in my life. Is it realistic to expect that on top of everything else I am looking for, there is someone who can make me feel at ease and let me be myself?*

What was it about me that would not allow a man to see me for my true self? I remember taking the Myers Briggs Type Indicator (MBTI) three times: during college, at my first job, and on my own later. MBTI is a personality test that reveals a person's preferences on four scales based on C. G. Jung's theories. I always scored right in the middle of all four scales. When I received my first result in college, I worried: *Is my test result inconclusive? Do I not have a type?* I spoke to my management professor about it.

"Being in the middle is not bad," he said. "It just means

that you are agreeable to both sides of your personality. For example, an extrovert will think you are an extrovert, same as her or him. And introverts will think you are one of them too." Based on the result of the MBTI, it seemed easy for other people to project their types onto me. I remembered that conversation with my professor clearly, but I didn't think I understood the impact that would have on my relationships because of this tendency to be "in the middle" and what that said about my identity and who I was at my core. I'd been told in the past by Michael that I was like a chameleon—changing based on whose company I kept.

During my last weekend visiting Ted, he got a call from the hospital; they needed him to go in right away. It was an emergency. He told me he wasn't sure when he'd be finished and asked if I wanted to go home. Since I didn't have any plans in Boston, I figured I'd just keep my bus ticket and stick to my original plan. He ended up working the entire weekend and took a break only to take me to the bus stop when it was time for me to go. I could feel the mood between us change from light to heavy. We said a quiet goodbye.

A few days later, he called me for the first time. "Hey, I think you're great. But I think you should see other people. You deserve someone who can spend time with you. Also, it would make me look good if you have other men around, you know?" He tried to make a joke out of it. I didn't understand why I would want to make him look good in that way. But I understood our relationship was over.

I had really liked Ted—he was smart and funny, and we had endless things to talk about. But looking at him more objectively, there were signs we didn't have a future: He hated Hillary and Obama, Bernie and Warren. He said he'd never marry again and was still in the middle of a messy divorce, which I didn't know until later, when he kept telling me his marriage was definitely over. I constantly debated with myself whether this meant that technically I was dating a married man. Another first for me. I came to see that he was in and out of relationships quickly. Objectively, he seemed destructive. After Ted, I avoided men who were separated, divorcing, or recently divorced.

Rachel told me again and again, "He's not a nice person." I wasn't sure I was with her on that. I thought about Ted often. I felt like we were compatible both mentally and physically. But I told myself to stop thinking about him unless he contacted me again and had finally gotten a divorce. Every few months, we'd text each other to check in. Through those texts, I found out he had a local girlfriend; then they broke up; then he moved in with someone else; then he moved out. The divorce was finally over. I stopped texting and checking in on him. It was clear we were done.

With Ted, I felt the chemistry from the very start. It was good to be reminded of what was possible when you would make that kind of connection. I remembered having the same feeling with Chris a long time ago. If someone liked me, I could totally feel it. I kept reminding myself that meeting people should be fun. Dating is not a test. It's an opportunity for two strangers to meet and get to know each other better.

Remember when, as kids, we were all so innocent? I wanted to be that curious and have an open mind and heart. If the first few dates weren't fun, it would certainly be hard to share our lives together. I wanted to look forward to hearing about someone's life stories, his likes and dislikes, his ups and downs. My best frame of mind was being cautiously optimistic.

Rachel told me, "When I first met my husband, I was surprised at how easy it was after so many crappy dates. When you meet the right person, you will just know that it's right." I realized that's what happens when two people are compatible and share the same values. This was the only way to sustain a long-term relationship.

Recently, Rachel introduced me to a friend of her friend— someone a lot older than me, by some twenty years. Lee was nearly retired, while I still had a good ten to twenty years to go before considering retirement. We spent a few months together and enjoyed the summer going on hikes, to movies, and out to dinner. He took me to the aquarium; another time, we went to the movies and saw *Wonder Woman*. Lee appeared to like me and wanted to get more serious. I thought he'd be happy to take care of me and share a life together.

During one of my business trips to DC, I had some time away from him to think about what I wanted. When I came home, he was eager to see me. We made plans to meet for brunch at Barcelona Brookline. He thought he would drive to my place, and we'd walk to the restaurant together as we had done before. But I told him to meet me directly at the restaurant. He sounded surprised. He could sense something different.

I saw him walk toward me in the restaurant's outdoor seating area. "Are you okay?" I could see that he wondered why we hadn't met at my home.

"I'm fine. I ordered food already. Do you want to look at the menu?"

"No . . . no, thank you." He focused on me.

"Oh." I paused. I might as well get to the point. "I don't think we should see each other anymore."

"Why?" His face changed color.

"I don't feel *that way* about you. I'm sorry."

He looked at me. "I was going to tell you I want to get to know you better. I was respecting you. I was waiting before getting more intimate."

"That's not what I want." I looked down at my plate and then back to his face.

He looked very upset, got up, and walked off. I could feel the hurt. I sat there, ate the egg I ordered, paid quickly, and walked home. At the lobby of my building, I saw a note, "For Mindy," on top of a small box and a bouquet of flowers. It was the first time he gave me a gift and flowers.

To be fair to him, I had to tell him how I felt as soon as I knew what I thought of him. I didn't want to settle for someone I didn't feel attracted to. He felt more like an older brother or a young uncle to me. We never spoke again.

In six years of online dating, I got plenty of rejections and had said no to many men. After the online matches and working with matchmakers, after being stood up and asked for money, after hurting others and being hurt, I felt the need to better understand why I was spending time looking for and meeting single men. *Why am I putting myself through this? Why am I dating? Do I really want to date? Do I really want a man in my life? Do I want to get married?*

I realized I was still a romantic. I grew up reading *Pride and Prejudice* and *Jane Eyre*, watching *The Sound of Music*, and devouring romantic books and movies. I dated because I hoped to meet someone who could be my best friend for life, to whom I could tell everything, and with whom I could be myself. I no longer wanted biological kids of my own. Given my age, that was really not a choice anymore but had more to do with the reality of time running out. I didn't need to get married but understood the preciousness of someone willing to commit to me "till death do us part."

"You don't have to get married if you don't want to. There are many types of relationships. Like Woody Allen and Mia Farrow—at least when they first were together." Rachel reminded me of the benefit of meeting men in my mid-forties.

"Yes, I remember reading about a couple in New York City. They bought two different apartments right next to each other and lived separately. If they wanted to, they spent time together in one of their apartments—very interesting!" I paused for a few seconds. "I might be afraid to say that I want a life partner. I don't want to be unrealistic or greedy. I like my current mindset. I want to be content."

From age forty-one to forty-six, I met thirty-five men and got to know something about all of them. More importantly, I got to know myself—both who I am and the kind of partner that would make my life a better one. Luckily, I was happy being alone. I didn't have to be with someone in order to enjoy life. There was no deadline for my dating. *I could meet someone when I am ninety!*

My life went on merrily without a man. Also, with my chameleon personality and everything that I was looking for—compatibility in intellect, physical attractiveness, shared life values, good chemistry—I could see it would not be easy for me to find the right match. My past long-term relationships made me more confident in my judgment and in the idea that I had to find the right person to meet my needs. I met many men who were incompatible with me, and I had no desire just to be with someone. With the wrong person, my contented life could turn into something miserable. I imagined my happiness fading away in front of me, which scared me.

I once asked Rachel, when she was single, why she dated. "Because I don't want to be alone when I am sixty." I remembered how I felt with Chris at the end of our relationship. That emptiness in bed when we were together. Having someone in my life didn't automatically guarantee a happy existence.

I remained single because of me, not because of not meeting anyone but because of all the decisions I made waiting to meet the right person. I liked my life as it was.

19

GRASS ON THE OTHER SIDE

Rachel and I had long talks about life and everything messy that was part of it. Unlike romantic movies, which typically ended with a happily-ever-after kiss, marriage and relationships took work. I heard all about it from Rachel, who'd been married at this point for more than ten years.

"I'm still trying to get pregnant," she told me one day. "We're trying IVF. There are so many appointments, and the shots really mess me up. I also don't know if my next pregnancy is going to be as bad as the last one. I couldn't keep any food down and vomited every day."

Another time, she said, "I'm good. Just sleep-deprived. The baby wants to nurse every three hours. He's also not sleeping through the night. The only way he falls asleep is if I hold him. And his big brother wants attention. He's jealous of the baby. Just hard to juggle all that."

As the years passed, she continued to tell me about her challenges: "I'm so tired. Every day at five, I try to leave work. People stop by to chat, but I don't have time for such things. I have to rush home to make dinner for the kids. I don't know why, but everything with the teenage boys is a big fight.

Whatever I say, they just talk back and say, 'No' or 'Fine' and roll their eyes. There's no respect. And I haven't had a single minute to myself in days."

"I have to enroll my girl in ten different camps and classes. There is no aftercare at her school. I can't just leave her at home while I work. This is so expensive. I still have to figure out how to take her to all of that while I work from home."

"Having kids is hard. With my husband away so much, I feel like I'm a single mother, which is difficult. If I knew earlier in my life what I know now, I'm not sure I'd do it again. I know you thought about being a single mother. If you asked me now, I'd say, 'No, don't do it.' My little girl screamed at me the other day. She has highs and lows. I think she might have ADHD. She doesn't listen at all. She can't get along with the rest of her siblings. I am so scared, and I don't know what I can do."

"I have my in-laws for a few months. They don't have any friends nearby. I'm worried about them being antisocial and feeling isolated. I want them to be comfortable, but I don't know if I have extra energy to take care of more people."

"My husband doesn't do laundry, cook, or look after the kids. For some reason, it's just not in him. He travels so much for work. So I have to prepare three meals a day, seven days a week. I feel like a single parent, even though I am married. I don't know if I would get married again if I had the choice again."

"I love going to Maine for winter weekends, but my husband doesn't want to go. It makes every weekend so stressful. We argue. If we don't go to Maine, what are we going to do with the kids all weekend? There is so much negotiation every week. I am so frustrated."

"I can't meet for dinner next weekend. I'm so sorry. My boy has soccer practice and golf the whole weekend."

"My husband and I are not doing okay. We are considering therapy. We might get a divorce."

And then I remembered the different kinds of challenges I'd hear from Rachel before she met her husband and got married:

"I was sitting in my living room and felt so lonely. I really hope I meet someone soon. I want to have someone to go and do things with. What's wrong with me? Why haven't I met someone?"

"I spend so much time meeting and dating men. It's all-consuming. But I find none of them attractive or compatible. I don't know how I can fill this hole in my life."

"My parents ask me why I don't spend more time dating. They think I'm getting old and should get married and have kids soon."

I just listened. I didn't know any better. I probably couldn't do any better if I were in her shoes. Rachel and Michael had a different life than I did. The grass on the other side wasn't greener. Life for Rachel and Michael and my other friends was complicated. I had a simple life. I went to bed at 10 p.m. and got more than eight hours of sleep if I wanted. I had 100 percent control over my time. I didn't have to explain or negotiate anything. I could be spontaneous. I'd built a happy life on my own, and I treasured what I had.

20

FROM SALSA TO BENEFITS

While I was riding on the red line, a voice called out to me, "Hi!" I looked up. It was George, Rachel's Greek friend from Athens who took us out on his dad's sailboat for three days. *OMG.* I hadn't seen him since then. He told me he'd recently become single. I had to get off the T but said we should get in touch. A few days later, he did.

"I'm taking a salsa class. Any interest?" George texted.

"Sounds like fun. I've never taken a salsa class before," I said. "How coordinated are you?"

"I have two left feet."

"LOL. Why not? I'm in!"

I kicked off 2020 by signing up for a salsa class for three months. I didn't grow up with ballet or gymnastics—that was not how my family raised me. Instead, my most precious toy was a set of plastic screws and strips I could connect together to make things. I also had a simple plastic train set that went around and around in an oval. But dance was always in the back of my mind. I took a dance class at a gym once. Even though I didn't have any talent, I enjoyed it. That was why I thought, *Hey, why not?*

On the first day of classes, I showed up early for the beginner class at Rumba y Timbal Dance Company in Central Square. There were already two more advanced classes in progress. I thought, *What a simple and beautiful concept. Two people agreed on steps, and with his lead, two people created a dance.* I watched all of the skilled dancers in the room with envy. I felt energized and couldn't wait for the class to start. George walked into the studio on time, interrupting my thoughts. We said hello and hugged.

Then the class started. The instructor asked everyone to line up. I found a spot in a line. George stood next to me. Then the instructor started showing basic salsa steps: front and back, left and right, and side to side. He asked everyone to follow his command as he moved his feet in the front of the room. We practiced a few rounds of footwork. Then the instructor asked everyone to pair up. George and I looked at each other and naturally got together. We held hands for the first time. We were in each other's personal space, and it felt perfectly natural. We danced a few steps.

Then the instructor said loudly, "Rotate." Another man stood in front of me. Every three to five minutes, I got a new partner. The new gentleman looked at me and smiled. He introduced himself and held out his hands to take mine. On command, we stepped to the music. There was an older gentleman around my grandfather's age with whom I partnered. He was very sweet with a gentle touch that warmed my heart.

I liked the rotation, which made salsa dancing a social event for me and more than just a date with George. I tried to remember everyone's names but couldn't. I knew them by the way they danced. It was fascinating to dance with different men leading me around the room. They were of different ages, heights, and builds. Different energy levels. Different dancing styles. But everyone had the same goal: trying to nail the steps we'd just learned. Once in a while, George and I would look for each other in the room and check on one another. A couple of times, I caught George messing up a step and apologizing. He laughed, and I smiled.

When the instructor gave commands for the next move, it was three beats ahead of the first step of that next move. During the beginning of the third class, I was having trouble with my turns. For some reason, I got out of beat while my lead tried to turn me. The instructor came over to me. "Don't turn when you hear the commend. You are trying to lead. Don't. Finish the steps. Let him lead." *Oh, of course, I try to exert control.* I had to laugh at myself in my head. So I slowed down. I tried to read my partner's tempo. After another rotation, George and I were back to dancing with each other. After I still felt off, he said, "Let me lead. You are still trying to lead." It got better. Of course, I was not in the beautiful phase, but four classes later, I could do four different turns.

Salsa reminds me of having a conversation. Like so many things in this world, listening is so important. We live in a world of constant communication. We have so many different interactions with others through many different channels. But rarely do we really stop and listen to someone carefully and intentionally. I am no better. I wondered if I could dance salsa without someone giving commands—if I would understand my partner's intention and direction without any words. Wouldn't that be amazing?

After the class, George suggested grabbing something to drink: "Coffee or alcohol?" I was overheated from the dance. I voted for a nearby café. Even in the freezing weather, I got iced tea to cool down, while he drank hot tea. I asked him about his family and what he'd been up to since I'd last seen him. He asked how life was for me. We also talked about dating and past relationships. The last thing we talked about was that we desperately needed to practice outside of class if we wanted to keep up. I loved salsa. I liked how my 2020 had started.

I remembered that my friends were concerned when I told them about seeing signals from strangers and in my surroundings. My confused and delusional thinking at the time was influenced by my schizophrenia. I read into things too much because my brain was broken.

In this situation, I was learning how to read authentic signals from my dance partners. Nonverbal communication made salsa dance magical. Two people in close proximity moved with the beats of the songs. I was a woman taking on the role of a follower. As a follower, I needed to learn to read my leading partner's indicating gestures, his raising of the right or left hand or both, his body turning, and his hand pressing the back of my shoulder. Based on these gestures, I knew what he had in mind and what to do. We danced together with absolutely no words.

But good dancers, I believed, did more than just give and read signs. The basics involved making sure the steps were technically correct. Trust came to mind. I had no idea what the next step was going to be. But wherever a man led, I followed. There was a feeling of synchronicity. At the right moment, we both took our steps at the same time. We had the same sense of rhythm. The force between the two of us also had to be equal and balanced. I was fairly relaxed when I danced. But there was a need to hold my frame and exert the right amount of force or pressure on him so he knew I was there, and the two of us could then feel connected.

Leading and following aside, both dancers were equally critical, needing to do their part, or the dance would fall apart. Some men were more natural at leading than others. Through their body, frame, and contact, their signals were clearer. However, practice made perfect. I felt better the more I danced. Two people got to know each other better when they spent more time moving with the one goal of making a beautiful dance together.

A Taiwanese term comes to mind, *mòqì*, which Google Translate explains as "tacit understanding." The Taiwanese phrase sounds more beautiful to me than the translation. I would say two people had *mòqì* when they felt they were on the same page (about something or everything), and it seemed they could read each other's minds. They usually finished each other's sentences, for example.

After six classes and a few hours of practicing, I felt pretty good about my ability to pick up basic salsa steps, at least technically. Then to have another kind of experience, I went to a body isolation class and couldn't move my head, shoulders, or hip in isolation. Ha! This is what the Taiwanese say: There are people above people and mountains beyond the mountains. There was much more to learn. Creating a beautiful dance might be a lifelong pursuit. I couldn't wait to learn more.

George asked me what my favorite thing about salsa was. "Spins and turns," I said. For me, dancing salsa is about different ways to spin. For George, it's about how to lead with his arm movements, how to direct and spin a follower.

During the first eight classes, we learned eight beats of

steps one at a time. As we learned more steps, George and I stayed after class to practice so that we could keep it all straight. That worked until we moved to the next level of salsa, and the instructor introduced us to a longer sequenced set of steps.

Franklin instructed, "Start with a switch-switch and then transition into a *copa*." As I rotated and danced with different partners, there were more exclamations: "I am sorry," "Oops!" "Oh no!" I almost stepped on someone when we should have turned in the same direction to start the *copa*. My left hand and arm should have been relaxed, but I held my arm too high, which made it harder for my partner to give me the momentum to turn left. My turning steps were so big that my partner might have to run after me as I turned. Once in a while, I remembered to spot, which was looking at one place in the room when I turned, which caused me to finish my step one beat behind. There were so many things going on all at once in sixteen beats. But I have to say, the sequenced moves were challenging and fun for me. I wanted to get them right.

Thank goodness the instructors, Franklin and Liliana, didn't get tired of leading the class through each move step by step. Our mistakes were also met with humor. "You don't want to strangle your partner with your arm!" "Don't look down. We don't know what you are looking at," "This is above the hip—not lower, not higher."

George commented during our practice how amazing it was that someone had thought of these steps before us and passed them down through generations. We were just scratching the surface of salsa. I was excited about dancing to longer sequences but also fearful that my small brain wouldn't remember all of the move combinations.

George and I ventured to a couple of salsa socials outside

of classes. "Oh, man," we said to ourselves, "people are such good dancers." Knowing the steps was one thing. Being able to dance with passion was quite another. Experienced dancers transitioned from move to move effortlessly. They relied on their muscle memory and made it seem spontaneous. At this point, George and I needed to concentrate to direct our bodies to do the right thing. In some ways, George needed to do more thinking than I did since he had to lead. He had to decide what steps we were going to dance to. Every eight beats was a decision for him.

We ran into one of our classmates at a social. "Are you two together?" Sam asked. I had danced with him many times before. He was there with his wife.

"We're just friends," George clarified.

It had been a while since I'd made friends with a single man. Rachel didn't think single men and women could be friends at our age. But I disagreed. Salsa was the perfect vehicle for George and me to spend time together. We both enjoyed the classes and each other. Regardless of how much we fumbled, we were happy to use a different part of our brain and be brave enough to continue.

I would continue to dance to the tune of my life.

Friendship with George was on one end of the relationship spectrum; the offer to be friends with benefits was on the other end.

I met Oscar on Facebook's new dating site, Facebook Dating. He was an assistant professor at a college nearby and was eager to meet. Oscar and I had our first date on a Friday night at Athan's Bakery in Brookline. He drove almost an hour to meet me. I got to the café first. I grabbed a seat, held off on ordering anything, and waited. "I am here." My phone flashed a text from Oscar. I walked toward the entrance and looked for someone based on the photo I'd seen of him. I recognized him immediately.

"Hi," I said. He waved back at me. When I saw him walking, I immediately thought he looked great. We sat at a table facing each other next to the window. He didn't want to just sit. As we chatted, I could see him squirming. "Can we go for a walk?" It was dark and cold outside, but I said, "Okay."

As soon as we were outside, he said, "Can I hold your hand, please?" Then he spent the rest of the walk asking if we could go to my place.

I told him, "It's our first date. Let's take it slow." I didn't feel ready to be intimate with him because we'd just met. He was obviously disappointed. I didn't even let him walk me home.

I knew right away he was a physical person. For me, emotional and physical attractions are equally important. I like being intimate with someone and having sex if it feels right. As a woman, I believe I enjoy sex as much as men. Some women might have stricter rules about timing. For example, I'd been told all my life that I should delay having sex for as long as possible. I didn't have rules like that. Sex was just another way to get to know a man. I wanted to be with someone compatible with me in bed.

For the second date the next Friday, I agreed to invite Oscar over to my place. He said he wouldn't know how he felt about me until we had "tried each other in the bedroom." The sex turned out to be good. There was chemistry. But something was missing. Beyond the initial infatuation, I didn't feel the deeper caring I'd had for my other boyfriends, which could only come with time.

"So not looking for a relationship?" I asked Oscar while

we ate together for the first time at my small dining table. I'd cooked some barbecue steak and Napa cabbage. He ate everything.

"No, I'm not," he said softly. I wasn't absolutely sure about this from our initial messages before we'd met, but there were signs. Usually, if a man only wanted sex, I wouldn't bother to meet up. But I had made an exception for Oscar because I wanted to meet him, and I was curious about how good he was in bed. "You have a nice apartment, a great job, and seem to have very good friends. You're very lucky."

Oscar was clear. He wanted to be friends with benefits. I found him attractive and considered his proposal. What I didn't have in my life were companionship and intimacy. Oscar was offering intimacy without companionship. I considered this. I would have a sex life. He would come every Friday night. *Is this a plus to my life? Do I want this?*

On Sunday, I texted him. "It's snowing! Winter is here." I asked how his weekend had gone. He told me he was uncomfortable texting with me because it reminded him too much of his ex-girlfriend. He didn't like that feeling. *This is too close?* At the moment, I knew having a purely physical relationship with a man wouldn't work. I would mistake the sex for love eventually. I wanted someone emotionally available. I wanted love and caring, not just good sex. I wanted good mornings and goodnights, to talk about how his week was, to take a walk together, to discuss a book, to have coffee together, and everything else that happened outside of the bedroom. I wanted to share a life.

Oscar came over for a third date. I wanted to see if he would be more comfortable with me. He still focused on satisfying me in bed.

"I don't think I can keep doing just this," I said when we were getting dressed.

"You're a smart woman. It's the right thing to end it. I'll delete your number." He put on his shoes, getting ready to leave my apartment for the last time. I was surprised at how reasonably and easily he responded. *Good, we agree.*

For a whole night, I thought about how surprised I felt realizing I'd developed feelings for him—a guy I barely knew who was just good in bed. I told myself, *You can't tame a wild animal. He will always be wild.* I didn't want to be permanent with someone like that. I reminded myself of all that I had. It was easier to come back to my own life after briefly welcoming someone into my home.

Three months later, Oscar texted me out of the blue. "Can I come over?"

"What? I am confused. Did you change your mind?"

"No. But I don't want to be alone tonight."

"I am not the solution to your loneliness. Besides, what about what *I* want?"

"Good point. I know. But wouldn't it be nice to feel each other?"

"Pass. No thanks."

Like me, the men I met who were in their forties and fifties all had relationship histories. Some were divorced. Some had kids. Some had a busy work schedule and little time for anything else. Also, like me, they usually had a fixed idea of the lives they wanted to lead. George and Oscar were men at opposite ends of the spectrum. Oscar was straightforward and wanted a friend with benefits. I had to say no. George and I loved dancing together, but nothing more came of it. I was fortunate to have met other men in between those two ends.

I found myself and the single men I met standing our ground and taking turns saying no. *The heart chooses what the heart chooses.*

I did the math in my head: one plus one better be two or two plus and not one and a half or one. *Whoever this person is that I let into my life better be super awesome.* I didn't want to end up with the wrong man. Having someone was not better if it was not the right person. *Actually, I quite like my life as it is—single!* At forty-seven, I knew what I was willing to compromise on and what I wanted to keep unchanged. I had so much in my life with friends and work and travel, and companionship when I wanted it, that I didn't feel anything or anyone was missing.

HOME AT LAST

When I returned to Boston from Taipei, I wanted a quieter home. Michael owned a one-bedroom in Brookline that had just lost its tenant. "Do you want to rent my place?" *Of course.* Two years after leaving Back Bay, I found the open space in Brookline pleasant. Instead of young students, my neighbors were older professionals and families. I met most of my neighbors. I no longer needed to live among endless restaurants and bars and retail stores.

After renting and living in his apartment for a year, I looked for a place to buy. "Do you want to buy mine?" Michael offered.

"You don't want to keep your rental property?"

"The rent is not that great."

"I love your place. This is going to be the best purchase because I test drove it for a year already. How much?" Michael told me a number similar to what I'd found online in the area. "Okay."

"Wait, you're supposed to make a counteroffer." Michael laughed. I was buying a great place from a dear friend, and I knew he was fair.

Setting up my new home this time was very different from

the one I'd put together in Back Bay ten years ago. I took my time and bought only the essentials. I no longer imagined throwing an eight-person, fancy sit-down dinner party. I'd used the huge dining table at my Back Bay place maybe five times in eight years. Now I had four silverware settings. I kept my friend's old—but beautiful—small, round table. I spent time putting up pictures of family and friends. I hung a sign that said "Less Stuff. More Life." I renovated the bathroom and installed new windows. I wanted all my clothes to fit into the closet and refused to buy a dresser. However, since I listened to music all the time, I splurged on Sonos speakers. But I still didn't own a TV.

"Stick to what you love," I said to myself.

I sat in my living room, trying to picture a man in my apartment. *Is that better? Would I be happier with a man?* I wasn't sure. I wouldn't have all the space to myself. *Am I selfish? Am I controlling?* I didn't think so. Where would his stuff go? There was no extra space in my apartment. We would need to get a bigger place and leave the home that I loved. My thoughts jumped around. Would he cuddle next to me while I read and wrote? Would he demand to get a TV? Would he make me watch sports and go to the gym to work out every day? What about dinners? *Will I have to cook for him every meal? Pick up his dirty laundry? What if he yells or, worse, hits?* The way I lived now, I could eat at any time I wanted and do anything I wanted to do whenever I wanted to do it.

Two months after I started taking salsa, in March 2020, the COVID-19 pandemic hit Boston and the world. The governor recommended that everyone stay at home. No more dancing. Restaurants closed for a while. I no longer saw my friends or went out for dinners.

As a single person, I hadn't liked cooking for one. I didn't like the idea of spending an hour preparing and cooking food that would be summarily eaten in fifteen minutes. Then I'd have to clean up for another half hour. For convenience and pleasure, I always ate out.

Because of the pandemic, I had to spend all my time at home alone. I took up cooking as a challenge. My biggest problem was not knowing what to buy at the grocery store. To make it easier for me to cook at home, I decided to subscribe to a food-ingredient delivery service for a month. On Mondays, I received a box filled with what I needed to cook the dishes on their menu that week. I had no problem following directions. After four weeks, I was ready to buy my own food. After summer, I had a routine: Trader Joe's for frozen food. Whole Foods for fresh food. Star Market for snacks. The Japanese market for Asian ingredients. I also stopped cooking one meal at a time and made them in larger quantities.

Rachel gave me a bread recipe and told me, "This is super easy. Even I can make it." I searched for flours and yeast for a few weeks because there was a shortage. When I finally found them, I baked bread that day. I used my oven for the first time. The smell of the fresh bread filled the apartment. I cut a piece to taste and added butter, and it made my mouth water. I ate a few more slices before freezing the rest. I baked the bread recipe three more times that summer. The kitchen was finally in full use.

I also thought this was a good time to relearn the piano and bought a keyboard. My aunt Theresa had been a piano teacher. As soon as I could sit up, she put me in front of a Yamaha piano. Every day, I had to practice for an hour. Because of her, I knew how to read notes. When I told her I was getting a keyboard, she got very excited. "A piano can be your best friend for life." As soon as it was delivered, I tried to play a sonata. I discovered my older fingers didn't listen to me as well as when I was a little kid. I would have to start with something easier. I hoped one day I could play songs and sing them in my own living room.

"I don't know if I need someone in my life. I'm pretty happy," I said to Rachel one day over Zoom.

"Single or not, I'm glad you're happy."

"I'm taking a break from dating. Instead of making an effort and spending money, I'm going to be serendipitous about it. Besides, pandemic dating is very awkward."

A pandemic was a true test of how I felt about my home and being with myself. In the morning, I got up and felt thankful for having a comfortable bed to sleep in. From nine to five, I worked remotely. Mixed in with meetings with coworkers all over the United States, I might also talk to or text with Dad, other relatives, and friends. Then I'd spend time cooking and eating. I might play the piano for a bit. At night, I read or watched something online. On weekends, I wrote, working on this memoir. At night, I took a hot shower, cleaned my apartment, and got ready for bed. I had a roof over me. I felt lucky. The pandemic made me look harder inside myself, and I found I had everything I needed.

EPILOGUE

I have fully embraced singleness and am happy with myself. There's nothing I want to do that I can't do by myself. I live life as a minimalist. I have myself and just what I need. I don't own a TV or a car. I dance in the middle of my living room when a good song comes on. Alone, I can sing along with my Spotify playlist and never feel embarrassed. My small home is safe and private and more than enough space just for me. I live on my own schedule with my independent will and total freedom. Feeding one mouth feeds the whole family. I splurge on friends, family, books, and travel. My friends keep me centered and joyful; I feel lucky to have so many good ones near and far. There are endless dinner dates and weekend brunches, glamping, swimming, hiking, weddings, and baby showers. I have a full life. As such, I never feel alone or that I'm missing something or have something wrong with me that might lead me to desperately want a boyfriend or husband.

Looking back on my life, I can't say I planned out every step. What I can say is that I've tried to live each day the best that I could, as if it were the last day of my life. My steps have led me to this day and to this person I have become, a single woman with a full heart.

Looking ahead, I am going to a wedding in Hawaii this summer.

Reply to the invite: Yes.

Number of guests: One.

I'm with me.

ACKNOWLEDGMENTS

In early 2019, the idea to write my second memoir was born. When some skeleton material was written, Elizabeth Brinsfield and Tracy Quinn McLennan gave me their honest first impressions. There was not enough there, and I had to work on it more. When I had a fuller draft, my four female beta readers—Mehek Bapna, Sofia Bapna, Wendy Shieh, and Maria Mutch—provided valuable critiques, validated my message, and encouraged me to continue. Elizabeth Brinsfield, my developmental and copy editor, helped me transition from a rough draft to a cohesive story with better clarity. Lastly, Hilary Crist, my final editor, helped me pull it all together into the final structure, form, and shape. Thank you all for being part of my writing journey.

To my Rachels, Michaels, and family, I am grateful and blessed to have you in my life. Without you and your love, I wouldn't be able to tell this story.

ABOUT THE AUTHOR

Mindy Tsai is an American memoirist. *I'm with Me* is her second memoir. She writes from her perspective of living as a single adult for twenty years. *Becoming Whole* was her debut book. She has schizophrenia and writes from her own personal experiences with the disease. She blogs on her website, mindytsai.com, focusing passionately on schizophrenia, dating, and writing, and she sometimes includes short stories.

Mindy was born in Taipei, Taiwan, and moved to New York City when she was a teenager. Her professional background is rooted in mathematics and science. She earned degrees in electrical engineering and engineering management at Cornell University. She is currently a manager for the digital health consultancy Medullan in Somerville, Massachusetts. She lives in Brookline, Massachusetts, where she enjoys food, books, walking, and writing.

Made in the USA
Monee, IL
31 October 2021